CHRISTMAS TREES
LIT THE SKY

CHRISTMAS TREES
LIT THE SKY
Growing Up in World War II Germany

Anneliese Heider Tisdale

authorHOUSE®

AuthorHouse™
1663 Liberty Drive
Bloomington, IN 47403
www.authorhouse.com
Phone: 1-800-839-8640

Author's Note: Some of the names in this book were changed for the sake of clarity or privacy. The names of family members were kept the same.

Published by AuthorHouse   10/30/2012

ISBN: 978-1-4772-7821-5 (sc)
ISBN: 978-1-4772-7820-8 (hc)
ISBN: 978-1-4772-7819-2 (e)

Library of Congress Control Number: 2012918859

Dedication

This book is dedicated to my children,
Larry, Linda, and Lorena,
who urged me many times to write the story of my life in
Germany.
I also want to thank their spouses,
as well as my "bonus" children,
Gary, Terri, Kirt, and Kent, and their spouses
for their love and support.
This book also is dedicated to my grandchildren,
Tonya, Trent, Nathan, Ian, Jessi, and Tessa,
and to my "bonus" grandchildren and
great-grandchildren,
who have given me so much joy.

Contents

Acknowledgements

First and foremost, I am deeply grateful to the late Dorothy Hannon for encouraging me to write this memoir. I would visit her on Thursday afternoons to read her portions of my manuscript. Dorothy, who was almost blind, would listen, ask questions, and give me feedback. She, along with my children, helped convince me that my story was worth telling.

Secondly, my sister-in-law Beverly Tisdale, a retired college English professor, read every page of this book. She taught me about transitions and other points about writing. I feel as honored and as lucky to have had her guidance as her students must have felt in her classrooms.

I also wish to thank Mary Sharp, whom I met at the Cedar Rapids Literary Club and who has become my dear friend. She edited this manuscript and provided the final spur to get this book published.

And last but not least, I gratefully acknowledge my husband, Jim Tisdale, for his unflagging and unconditional love and support, not only for this book but for everything I do. Thank you, Jim.

Chapter 1

The Surrender of Munich

Youth has the resilience to absorb disaster
And weave it into the pattern of its life,
No matter how anguishing the thorn
That penetrates its flesh.

—Sholem Asch

April 1945. Germany is in the last throes of World War II. Hitler's orders are to defend every German city to the last man.

My parents and I live on the outskirts of Munich. For weeks now, we have known it would not be long until our fate would be decided. Would Munich be allowed to surrender, or would we be forced to fight "to the last man," as the *Führer* had ordered?

Like the other residents in the area, my parents and I had been hoping and praying that the American Army and not the Russians would liberate Munich. Outrageous atrocities by the Russians against the civilian population in the eastern part of Germany had been reported. Women and girls had been repeatedly raped. Attempting to escape their pursuers, they often jumped out of windows to their death.

I was 17 years old.

It was a time of chaos, of living from day to day and hour to hour. During the last few days, we had seen many retreating German soldiers and SS coming through the suburb of Munich where we lived. Some of them were just boys who, at the last moment, had been stuck into a uniform and received the SS tattoo. They slept on the ground in a field close to our house and on the lawns of the neighboring houses, eating whatever they had left of their emergency rations. Some had stopped by our house and asked to fill their canteen with water before trudging on. Tired and bone weary, their uniforms looked like they had been worn too long. The soldiers seemed to be heading south, toward the safety of the mountains. Each one of them was someone's father, husband, son, or brother. Our hearts ached for them, but we also feared that, with them here and the Allied forces approaching so fast, we would be caught in the middle of the fighting.

During these last days of the war, no one was too young or too old to die for Hitler. A few days earlier, men, too old to serve in the army, were inducted into the *Volkssturm,* the People's Militia. Unlike my cousin Mariele's father, my father was exempted, having lost his right arm in World War I. These men were issued guns and told by the local party leaders to position themselves in the ditches along Landsberger Street. Their orders were to shoot once the American troops approached. While they didn't dare say anything to openly disobey that order, they also made no plans to follow it.

On April 28, 1945, the resistance group *Freiheitsaktion Bayern,* Freedom Action Bavaria, stormed two radio towers in Munich. Their broadcasts urged people to fly the Bavarian flag instead of the swastika and to hang out the white sheet of surrender to save Munich from total destruction and extra bloodshed. When the resistance group was no longer able to hold the radio towers, its members had to flee. Those captured were executed on the spot.

We were alone in our house again. Baroness von B. and her daughter, who had been assigned two rooms in our house after being bombed-out during the 1943 air raids in Hamburg, had left several days ago. With the battle for Munich approaching, they felt safer with relatives in the mountains.

Fräulein Kern, the young woman who had also occupied a room in our house, had left yesterday after work to face the end struggle with her family. The house suddenly seemed silent and empty.

We decided it was time to try and prepare for any fighting, shelling, or bombing. All day we methodically carried food, water, blankets, cots, and clothing down into the basement. We could not anticipate what the next few days would bring, and we felt frustrated and anxious.

Papa had a white sheet ready. He minced no words telling Mama and me that no one but he was to hang out the white sheet. *I hope he knows when the time is right,* I thought. *If he hangs it out too soon and there are any SS around, they will hang him from the nearest tree. If he doesn't hang it out soon enough, the approaching American troops will most certainly shell anything they feel is hostile.*

For some time we had heard the big guns moving closer. Now the U.S. forces had given the city of Munich the ultimatum to surrender the city unconditionally, or it would be leveled to the ground. Their bombers stood ready. Tomorrow would be decisive. It was a waiting game, and we were the pawns.

We sat down to a small evening meal and ate in silence. After supper, I told my parents I was going out to gather some dandelion greens to feed our rabbits. We might not be able to feed them tomorrow. Picking up my basket and knife, I went outside.

My friend Erna and her brother, Theo, were standing in front of their house. I walked over to them.

"Have you heard anything? Will they surrender the city?" I asked, knowing it was a futile question.

Theo shrugged his shoulders. "No one knows, but by tomorrow this war'll be over for us, one way or the other."

"I hope the soldiers in the field over there move out, for their sake and ours. I'm just glad we aren't going to wind up in the hands of the Russians," I replied, my voice tight with emotion.

Erna nodded in agreement and said, "Anything has to be better than the Russians. I can't let myself think of that possibility. Are you sleeping in the basement tonight? That is, if there is to be any sleeping."

"No, we're staying upstairs till there's some shelling, but the basement is ready," I said and added, "I need to get some more rabbit food. Want to come? It won't take long."

We started picking the dandelions that grew along the roadside. It was a relief to be outside, to keep busy, and to talk with Erna. In the house I had felt like screaming.

During the night, I slept sporadically. Sometime after midnight, I heard the German soldiers move out, and I was relieved. *I don't want to see any more fighting, people dying, and for what? The war is over, it's only a matter of a few days . . . no more blood . . . . Just let it all be over.* I thought of my brother Ludwig, a prisoner somewhere in Russia. Was he still alive? *Please, dear God, be with my brother and guide him back to us safely. Mama desperately needs her son back. I don't think she can survive without him.* My pillow was wet with tears when I finally went back to sleep.

The morning of April 30 dawned. It looked like it would be a nice spring day, no rain and not too cold. Up much earlier than usual, we no longer heard the big guns. Were they getting ready to bomb Munich to the ground? The absence of the usual morning activities resulted in an eerie silence. No one was rushing to get to work. No one was out shopping for milk or warm hard rolls for breakfast. There were no vehicles in the street, no children playing or walking to school. It seemed that even the birds forgot to sing. It was too quiet—a silence so strange, unnatural, and menacing, it sent a chill down my spine.

My parents decided not to retreat to the basement until necessary. Papa took the white sheet and went up to the attic so he could see the street leading to the city of Landsberg, from where the U.S. troops would approach.

After a while, he called for Mama and me to come up, too. We had just installed ourselves by the attic window when the deadly silence was broken by a gradually increasing rumbling noise. This was a new sound, not like the deep drone of approaching aircraft. We were facing a new danger. Not knowing what form it would take was frightening.

This is the Heider house in Munich, Germany.

This is the Heider family in 1938, before World War II.
From left: Ludwig, Mama, Anneliese, and Papa.

Soon the source revealed itself as we stared at the first American tank turning off Landsberger Street. Just to look at its massive bulk was intimidating. It looked like nothing could stop it. To imagine the destruction its guns could inflict terrified me.

Papa felt this was the time, and he rushed to hang out the white sheet from the attic window, where it was clearly visible to the approaching American troops. There was very little shooting, only the occasional crack of a rifle. By now, the first tank was rolling down Main Street with another one approaching in the distance.

Alongside each tank, foot soldiers walked with guns ready to fire. I felt like everything around me was surreal, yet it was very real. *Is this it? Have they surrendered the city? They won't bomb us with their tanks already here.* I looked at the tanks and the soldiers. *They are all the way from America where my grandmother and Mama's sister, Aunt Katherine, and Cousin Joey live. Could one of these soldiers be my relative?*

I wanted to see their faces, but their helmets and chinstraps were in the way. Checking their uniforms, my eyes finally focused on their boots. They looked strange. The pant bottoms were bloused and tucked into their boots. I had never seen soldiers, or anyone else, with the bottom of their trousers stuck into their boots. In the midst of this grave situation my eyes focused on something as insignificant as the boots. The picture of the tank, the foot soldiers, and the boots is still clear in my mind today, more than 65 years later.

Is the war really over for us? I couldn't believe it was. Six long horrible years, and now what? *We don't have to be afraid of the Russians anymore . . . . There'll be no more bombing . . . . But what will this occupation be like? Where is Ludwig? Will the Russians release their prisoners of war and let him come home? Will our family be whole again . . . happy like before the war?*

All of these unanswered questions raced through my young mind. I wasn't sure what I felt or if I was capable of feeling anything. It was like I was in a vacuum. Papa's voice interrupted my thoughts, "It looks like everyone is surrendering. I believe the fighting here is over. Let's go downstairs and listen to the radio. Maybe there are some announcements."

Much later, we found out that Karl Fiehler, the mayor of Munich, along with Paul Giesler, the much feared Nazi leader of the Bavarian district, and other high party members in command of the city had fled Munich. The city was without a government, had become a no man's land. The city was now able to surrender, but with all the high officials gone, who was there to sign the document of surrender? Finally, one of the city clerks was located. Ironically, it was this lowly scribe's last official act to surrender Munich, the city of a million people, the capital of Bavaria, to the Americans.

This picture was taken in 1944 when I was 16 years old.

This picture was taken in our yard in Munich.

The radio was issuing instructions for everyone to stay indoors and not to resist the advancing American troops.

We hadn't eaten anything yet this morning, so now Mama made coffee, and we had a light breakfast. The radio broadcast strict orders to stay indoors and to listen for further instructions. Curfew times would be announced later. It was like we were in a trance. The war was really over for us!

Breslau, the city on the Oder River, was not so lucky. Breslau was not allowed to surrender but was forced to fight on. The end for Breslau didn't come until May 6, 1945, when it finally surrendered to the Russian Sixth Army, after a siege of 82 days. Its men and women had to pay a horrible price for Breslau's desperate defense. The brutality brought to the inhabitants of this city was unheard of. In the Russian-occupied sector of Germany, approximately two million women were raped. It was perhaps the largest mass rape in the history of the world.

On May 5, Germany's Army Group G surrendered to the U.S. Sixth Army in Bavaria. We were defeated. Hitler's dictatorship and his "Thousand Year Reich" were over. They ended after unbelievable human suffering, in the rubble of European cities, after the deaths of millions of soldiers, men, woman, and children from all the countries involved.

We are now a conquered people. But for me, on April 30, with the surrender of Munich, I feel only a sense of unreality and relief. Then I look at Papa with his wooden right arm that replaced the one he lost during the Great War in France in 1916. Now, his son—my brother, Ludwig—is missing in action in Russia. For my parents, this is the second war they have had to live through. I can't help but wonder will I, too, have to face another war? Will I have children who have to go to war? I don't voice these daunting questions because I know there is no one who can answer them.

Several hours after the U.S. troops occupy the city, I cautiously look out the window. Because of the curfew, I can't go outside, but I can open the window. It has turned into a nice day. The air smells fresh and clean and, for the first time in days, I notice the spring flowers in Mama's carefully tended flower bed, the only one that had not been spaded up to raise vegetables. Our fruit trees are budding, some are in bloom. The eternal renewal of nature.

Can we renew ourselves? Is it possible that people, however scarred, come back from all of this . . . ? I was eleven years old when this nightmare started, now I'm seventeen. Years lost to the war—my youth lost to the war. Somehow, we survived, and I pray that somewhere in Russia my brother is alive and will come home to us. Mama always says tomorrow is another day. I have to hold on to that thought.

My thoughts drift to World War I, to my father lying mortally wounded on the battlefield in France . . . .

Chapter 2

A Difficult Beginning

France, January 1916. The fighting between the German and French troops in the woods of Givenchy had been heavy. On January 28, 1916, Martl Heider of the 3rd German Infantry Regiment was carrying a wounded soldier on his back when a grenade hit nearby, killing the wounded man and tearing off Martl's right arm just below the elbow.

Of his left hand, only the mangled stumps of the pointer and middle finger remained. The only semblance of a fingernail poked out of his gnarled left thumb. His warm blood was seeping into the cold earth.

Clinging desperately to consciousness, his mind screamed unrelentingly *you can't die here . . . . you can't die here . . . .* With adrenalin flowing, he stumbled back toward the safety of the German lines but collapsed shortly before reaching them.

My story actually starts here, on this battlefield in France. Martl Heider is destined to be my father.

For his efforts in rescuing wounded soldiers from the battlefield, Martl received the *Silberne Tapferkeitsmedallie,* Silver Medal of Bravery, *the Militär Verdienstkreuz,* Military Service Cross, and the *Eiserne Kreuz,* Iron Cross.

During a long convalescence and rehabilitation, Martl learned to function with two prostheses for his right arm. His dress arm had a leather glove over a wooden hand; the other prosthesis was for work. Into it, he could insert a hammer, a screwdriver, or a metal ring for holding a rake, hoe, or shovel. With what remained of his left hand, he learned to write and eventually became an accomplished lefty.

Before the war, Martl had worked for the railroad as a carpenter, outfitting sleeping car compartments. After his convalescence, the railroad retrained him to work in their administrative offices in Munich, where he took care of the incoming and outgoing mail and dispatched it to numerous departments within the vast building.

My mother, Elisabeth, although not having suffered through a traumatic experience like my father, had not had an easy childhood. Apprenticed to a laundry in Traunstein, she was forced to carry heavy buckets of water and scrub laundry on a washboard from morning till night, for little more than room and board. It was a job much too hard for a thirteen year old, a job with no chance for advancement, no chance to better her life.

Elisabeth's Aunt Therese, her mother's sister, searched relentlessly and was finally able to find employment for Elisabeth in Munich with the Baroness von Bechtoldsheim. The baroness, a kind and generous person, soon recognized Elisabeth's ability and arranged for her to become an apprentice in the kitchen of Count Wrede in Munich. Elisabeth, appreciative of this opportunity, was a good and eager student who was soon able to create savory dishes and elegant desserts for the count's table.

Upon completion of her apprenticeship, Elisabeth became a cook on the staff of Baroness Marogna von Redwitz in Munich. On her afternoon off, Elisabeth always looked forward to visits in the home of her Aunt Therese and Uncle Georg in Munich. She always felt welcome and loved in the home of these two people, who treated her like a daughter and encouraged her thirst for knowledge by lending her books and by sometimes taking her to the theater or a concert.

Elisabeth was very close to her only brother, Franz Xaver, who was with the German Army near Givenchy, France. Whenever Elisabeth received a letter or card from him, it seemed like a holiday to her. In his last card, dated January 1, 1916, he thanked her for a package of food and brandy she had sent him. He wrote: "The brandy really warms my innards .... There hasn't been any fighting. We have been standing together with the Frenchmen all day, smoking and trying to talk ...."

War is insane. They don't want to fight, but on command, when the battle starts, they have to kill each other. What for? Who can order one person to kill another? I'd like to put all the top brass who want war in one room to fight it out, then there wouldn't be any war .... Elisabeth despised the war with her innermost being.

A few weeks later, Elisabeth received the news that her brother had been killed with a single shot to the forehead. She was devastated.

Two years later, the war ended with the defeat of Germany. The newly formed Weimar Republic was weak and plagued with political unrest and social instability. In May 1921, prices started rising rapidly and by July 1922, prices had escalated 700 percent. The value of the German mark fell by the hour.

Employees who had been paid monthly now were paid weekly, then daily. Workers rushed home after being paid with a backpack full of paper money and hurried to buy what they could because in a few hours the marks would buy only a fraction of what they could buy at the moment.

Prices rose so rapidly that the cost of a meal in a restaurant increased while the diners were eating. By 1923, the 1,000 mark bill was overstamped in red to read 1 billion. It took 200 billion marks to buy one loaf of bread. Ordinary postage stamps had overprints of thousands, then millions, and finally billions of mark. It was runaway inflation, hyperinflation.

To add to the economic woes, a demand was made that Germany repay the money it had been loaned after the war within 90 days. This was an ultimatum Germany could not possibly fulfill. Businesses closed, and people lost their jobs.

It was in this context that my parents started their married life.

Elisabeth had met Martl Heider at the home of her Aunt Therese and Uncle Georg. Within a year, they were engaged, and they married six months later, on November 29, 1919, in Munich.

Elisabeth Bernauer and Martl Heider,
my parents, on their wedding day in Munich.

They were a handsome couple, but like most pictures of that time, their wedding picture shows them looking stern. They moved into an apartment in a suburb of Munich. Since the apartments were subsidized by the railroad, they were affordable. The inhabitants of each apartment also had a small fenced-in garden plot in back of the buildings.

A year after they were married, their son, Ludwig, was born. They were grateful and happy to have a healthy son, even though it meant another mouth to feed and another body to clothe. Times were hard. It was a daily challenge just to put food on the table and to pay the bills. Probably because he had worked for the railroad before the war, was a disabled veteran, and a dependable worker, Martl was able to keep his job. Elisabeth was a good manager. Food prices were exorbitant, but she found ways to feed her family. Many days Elisabeth went to the butcher's and bought only beef bones from which she would make a hearty soup. Her earlier training as a cook helped her use the less expensive organ meats—such as heart, liver, tongue, and kidneys—to make tasty dishes.

When those economies failed, and they might have gone hungry, their garden rescued them. Every inch of the garden plot was used for potatoes, vegetables, strawberries, gooseberries, and currants. A small kitchen garden was filled with chives, parsley, borage, sage, dill, and summer savory. Peppermint and chamomile were planted for tea.

Reluctantly, but motivated by love, Martl gave up a small corner of the valuable garden area so Elisabeth could plant a few flower seeds one of the neighbors had shared with her. Elisabeth loved flowers and, during the summer, a few freshly cut flowers always graced the table at mealtime.

This is my brother, Ludwig.
He was eight years old when I was born.

Ludwig was in grade school and almost eight years old when I was born. My parents named me Anna Elisabeth <u>Anneliese</u>. Anneliese was underlined on the birth certificate because that was to be my "calling name." Now my parents had the daughter they had hoped for to complete their family.

Elisabeth had never come right out and said so, but Martl knew she longed to have some "good dishes" for holidays and special occasions. At the department store in Munich, he had seen her run her hand gently over a pretty cup or plate. Martl stringently saved some money and bought a set of white dishes with scrolled edges and pink roses. They would be ideal for the christening of their little girl.

My mother often told the story of my christening and of what would turn out later to be my troubled beginnings. Aunt Therese, Uncle Georg, Aunt Martha, and her daughter, Julie, my godmother, came to the christening at the local church. In my pretty white christening dress, I slept peacefully through most of the ceremony, until the cold holy water hit my forehead, when I let everyone know what a good set of lungs I had.

Elisabeth pinched the household budget to be able to provide a special meal after the christening. Thanks were given for the health of the mother and the new arrival. It was a joyous afternoon, with me passed from one relative to another.

My troubles began several months later when Mama stopped nursing me after her milk supply gave out. She then put me on cow's milk, but every time I was fed a bottle of cow's milk, it would not be long until I would vomit it up in one great gush, and soon start to cry and fuss again with hunger.

My parents realized they had to find something fast to give me the nourishment I needed. They knew of a farmer who raised goats and sheep along with the usual livestock. Intent on finding a solution, Papa rode his bicycle into the country and told the farmer of their plight. The farmer was glad to help and sold him some sheep's milk, but the same thing happened: I could not keep it down. Goat's milk produced the same discouraging result.

Elisabeth and Martl were frantic, worried that they would lose their little daughter. Since Mama had stopped nursing me, I wasn't gaining enough weight and fretted day and night. They had to find something that would agree with me, and they needed to find it fast in order to keep me alive.

One day my family was having their noon meal. According to custom, it was the large meal of the day and, during the week, it started with soup. Mama held me in the *Wickelkissen*, a type of baby bunting. I had regurgitated my last bottle and was crying pitifully with hunger. In desperation, Mama gave me a spoonful of soup broth. They tell me that I hungrily slurped it up and, in order to keep me quiet, Mama fed me several more spoonsful. It seemed as if I knew my life depended on it; I hungrily swallowed it and cried for more.

Fifteen minutes passed, then half an hour. Everyone was done eating, and I still kept the soup down. Mama added some farina to the broth, fixed a bottle, and fed it to me. They waited with bated breath, but I kept the soup down and soon fell asleep.

In the following weeks, I seemed to do well with the various broths and soups Mama fixed for me. Mashed vegetables were added, and it was noticeable that I was gaining weight. By the time I was a year old, I actually had acquired some "baby fat."

My own beginning, like that of my parents, certainly had been anything but easy, and the future and another war would test our ability to survive again and again.

Chapter 3

Early Adventures

Some of my earliest recollections are from the time we lived in the apartments on Aubingerstrasse. Because shopping in one of the big department stores in Munich was less expensive and there was more variety than in the suburb where we lived, Mama took the commuter train every four to six weeks to shop for special things in Munich. She often took Ludwig and me along and treated us to lunch in the restaurant of the Tietz department store.

On this particular day, Mama and I went to the city while Ludwig was in school.

As usual, the department store was crowded. Mama told me to hang on to her skirt so she could look at some kitchen towels. I could not see to the top of the counter. Wedged in between all of the shoppers, I could hardly breathe. Then I remembered all the toys and especially the big brown bear I loved to ride the last time we were here. It was not long before I started out to find the toy department.

"Where are you off to in such a hurry, little Miss? Are you lost?" a lady at one of the cash registers asked me.

"No, I'm going to ride on the brown bear," I answered.

"What's your name?"

"Anneliese . . . . I have a big brother. His name is Ludwig . . . he already goes to school."

The salesclerk was no longer listening to me and soon the intercom was blaring: "Little Anneliese is waiting at cash register 18 for her Mommy."

Mama was very upset when she came to pick me up.

"Why did you run away? You were very naughty."

"I just wanted to ride on the big bear."

"I told you we had to do some shopping first. Now take my hand and don't let go."

Mama grasped my hand and, while she finished her shopping, she hung on to my hand with an iron grip.

When we were home, Mama told Papa about that little episode and added: "When I got to the cash register to pick up Anneliese, she was happy as a lark. She had not shed a tear. Ludwig would have been crying his eyes out when he was her age. I think from now on I'll leave her with Frau Reisach so I can get my shopping done."

Even at age four-and-a-half, I look ready for adventure.

The Reisachs lived in the apartment above us. Herr Reisach was a very kind and gentle man, while Frau Reisach was a high-spirited and resolute woman with heavy, honey-colored braids that encircled her head. Not having any children of their own, the Reisachs doted on Ludwig and me. Frau Reisach didn't seem to mind that I was too rambunctious, as Mama called it. With Ludwig in school, she showered all her attention and love on me. She always had time to go on walks with me, sometimes with my doll carriage, my doll, and Teddy securely tucked in. Other times we walked in the nearby woods or meadow to look at butterflies, flowers, and leaves. She even let me pick up caterpillars and pretty stones.

On the way home, we often stopped at the pastry shop to pick up a piece of *Bienenstich,* a slice of cake with a cream filling and a gooey honey-almond topping, which we shared back home in Frau Reisach's kitchen. I relished the times I spent in Frau Reisach's care.

When it was time again to go shopping in Munich, Mama handed me a little, red-enameled pan: "I have put your favorite *Wurst* and a *Semmel,* hard roll, in here for your lunch." She admonished me: "Now promise me you'll be good and that you won't ask Frau Reisach for anything."

"*Ja,* Mama."

Mama rang the doorbell and, after a few words with Frau Reisach, she left for Munich.

The Reisachs' kitchen with the dark green-tiled *Kachelofen* was cozy and smelled wonderful with one of Frau Reisach's hearty soups simmering on the stove. Handing Frau Reisach my lunch pail, I started to settle down on the corner bench by the stove, when I saw "it" on the small table in the corner—a beautiful shiny bowl with an orange, a few apples, and a banana. *It must be silver, like Mama told me they had when she worked for those people in a castle.*

Südfrüchte, fruits from the south, had to be imported and were rather pricey. My parents were saving every penny they could to build their own home, so oranges and bananas were reserved for special occasions, such as St. Nikolaus Day.

I remembered my promise to Mama. I must not to ask for anything. The fruit looked tempting. I got up and walked over to see it up close and maybe even smell it.

"Should we share some fruit?" Frau Reisach asked.

19

I didn't know what to do. I knew I was not to ask for anything, but I was supposed to answer when asked, so I silently nodded my head yes.

"Which one shall we have?" was Frau Reisach's next question.

I pointed to the orange, and Frau Reisach peeled it, sectioned it, and put it on a little plate. We sat at the table eating the orange, and I savored every juicy bite.

"Thank you, *Bau Reitag*, now can we look at magazines?" Ever since I first started to speak and couldn't quite master saying *Frau Reisach,* it was *Bau Reitag* for me.

Frau Reisach belonged to a magazine service, so she always had the latest magazines with lots of pictures. I would point to a picture, and Frau Reisach would tell me the story behind the picture. I loved to hear about the little princesses, Elizabeth and Margaret, in England, about the child movie star Shirley Temple in America, where my aunt, Mama's sister, lived. I always was fascinated by stories about animals, domesticated or wild. I vividly remember a picture about birds on their migration to Africa being trapped in Sicily to be eaten. I got very upset and was adamant that someone had to stop this practice. I felt frustrated being little. I wanted to go there and stop them—whoever they were.

When Mama picked me up in the late afternoon, she asked Frau Reisach if I had been good and not asked for things. Frau Reisach answered yes on both counts. I was very glad that apparently Frau Reisach did not consider nodding and pointing as actually asking for something.

Frau Reisach always held a very special place in my affection, so much so that in later years whenever I came back to Munich to visit my parents, I always made sure to also visit Frau Reisach.

Chapter 4

The New House

Mama and Papa had been saving for a house with a yard for Ludwig and me. Every penny of Papa's *Invalidenrente*, disability pension, was faithfully put away each month, and my parents gave up many simple pleasures. Papa had never been a man to go to the tavern after work. He enjoyed a beer at home with his evening meal and limited himself to one cigarette a day, slowly savoring each puff while walking in the garden. Mama made do with a couple of good dresses, which she wore on alternating Sundays to church.

I was not yet four years old when their dream became reality, and they were able to build their own home. We moved into the two-story stucco house, with green shutters on the four windows in the façade. It sat back on a double lot, a wide drive leading up to it.

To me, our new house seemed like a castle, and I was the princess. I practiced walking down the curved stairway in one of my mother's old dresses, pretending it was an expensive gown. My imaginary guests looked up in admiration at my grand entrance. The new house became the setting for fantasies I created out of the stories Mama told me of life at the homes of the nobility where she had worked.

A friend and I pose with our doll carriages.

Upon entering the main door of the house, there was a red-tiled foyer that was never heated and served as cold storage since refrigerators or even iceboxes were unheard of. Beneath a large mirror, there was a built-in credenza where Mama kept eggs, lard, rendered beef tallow, clarified butter, big jars of her homemade pickles, and other needed items.

On each side of the mirror hung the stuffed head of a stag. Mama never was very fond of those deer heads, but I remember asking Papa to lift me up so I could pet them. Their eyes looked so soft and so sad, I wanted to cradle and comfort them.

From the foyer, a door led into the long hallway where, late in fall, Papa always put up an *Anthracit* stove. Because anthracite is a hard, clean-burning coal, this stove needed to be stoked only once every 24 hours. If we left our bedroom doors open, it would take the chill off when the weather got bitter cold.

From the hall, doors led into the kitchen, the living room, the half-bath, the extra bedroom, and to the basement stairs.

The kitchen was large. Besides cooking our food, the large wood-burning stove heated the *Rutscherl,* flatirons, for ironing, and the reservoir provided us with warm water. A large table with a corner bench served for eating our meals. The seats of the bench opened up and provided a lot of storage.

One of the most important items in our kitchen was a scale with a wooden block of weights because all recipes were given in pounds and grams, while liquids were measured in liters and milliliters.

In the corner next to the cupboards was a Singer foot-treadle sewing machine.

Along the wall was the sofa where Ludwig or I slept if we were sick, and where Mama sometimes allowed herself a short nap on Sunday afternoon.

In the far corner of the kitchen was a crucifix, usually adorned with palm fronds from the previous Palm Sunday. On the kitchen wall, to the right side of the door, hung a ceramic container for holy water. Whenever we left the house, or at night before she tucked us in, Mama would bless us by sprinkling holy water on our foreheads.

Next to the kitchen was our living room and study. There was a round table with four chairs, a sofa, and an oversized desk where Ludwig studied. The desk matched an enormous *Bücherschrank*, book cabinet, with two beautifully carved wooden panels on the side doors and a large glass center door. A prominent place in the bookcase held Ludwig's collection of Karl May books. Karl May was one of the most read young people's author of that time. He wrote about the American "Wild West" and foreshadowed the coming demise of the Indians and the vast herds of buffalo with the advance of the white man.

A short time later, a piano was added to the living room, and Ludwig started piano lessons.

From the central hall, a curved parquet stairway led up to the second floor. My bedroom was at the head of the stairs. It had a double window with sheer-white, tie-back curtains and small curtains on the window panes. Mama called the curtains *brise-bise,* which was actually a French term.

Now that I think about it, there were lots of French terms used by older people when I was little. I grew up with these terms and did not know they were not German words. The use of French terms in Germany went back to Frederick the Great of Prussia, who was enamored with the French language and used it in his court, *Sans Souci,* Without Care.

So, Mama sometimes admonished me to walk on the *trottoir,* sidewalk, or asked me to fetch her *porte-monnaie,* billfold. When saying goodbye, we'd say *adieu*. Our neighbors lived *vis-à-vis*, across from us. And when a girl had a date, she had a *rendez-vous*.

But thinking once again about my bedroom, I remember that on my bed I had a thick feather cover that was daily hung over the windowsill, along with the pillows, to air out. My room also had a small, dark-green tile stove in one corner, but it would be used only when the weather was bitterly cold or on holidays, when I sometimes played in my room while the adults visited.

At other times when the nights were cold, Mama filled our oval hot water bottles. Made out of metal, they were tied into cloth covers to keep them from burning our feet. They always got the beds cozy warm. A dresser, a wardrobe, a small table with a drawer for pencils, and a chair completed my bedroom.

Next to my bedroom were the bedrooms of my parents and Ludwig.

The door next to the bathroom opened to the attic stairs. The attic had half-round windows facing in each direction. From here, one could see the whole neighborhood and, on a clear day, the beautiful mountains of Bavaria, the Alps.

The attic served other purposes as well. It was the place where we stored Christmas decorations and seasonal items, where Mama dried fruits and seeds she harvested from the garden since the open attic windows provided good ventilation. It was where we kept flour, which my parents bought in bulk, along with a large round horsehair sieve for sifting the flour in a sturdy wooden chest. It was where, during the cold winter months, Mama often would hang the laundry to dry.

Like the upper floors, the basement also had a central hallway with doors leading to various rooms. There was Papa's workshop, his domain, where, to Mama's consternation, he oiled just about everything to keep it from rusting. Mama didn't like the oily smell nor the job of getting the oil stains out of his clothes on washday.

The workshop held Papa's large circular whetstone, operated by foot, which he used to sharpen tools, scythes, Mama's kitchen knives and scissors, and anything else that needed sharpening.

All the tools he needed to repair and maintain the house and its objects were in his workshop, and he prided himself about never having to call a workman to fix things. His reputation as a handyman was known so well that people in our neighborhood sought his advice if they had something to repair.

His workshop also reflected his frugal and meticulous nature. Nothing was wasted. If a nail was crooked, he straightened it and used it again. Everything had its place, and no one had better disturb that order. Ludwig got into trouble more than once when he failed to return things he had used for his experiments to their proper place.

The next basement door led to the *Waschküche*, laundry. Once a month, the night before washday, the dirty laundry was soaked overnight in big tubs of water to which *Persil*, a detergent, had been added.

Early the next morning, while Mama got breakfast ready, Papa filled the huge cement-encased cauldron with water and built a fire in the firebox underneath it. When breakfast was over, a hard bar soap, *Kernseife*, was cut into the water and the white wash was boiled.

A *Wäschestämpfer*, a bell-shaped device on a long handle with an inner smaller cylinder, was pushed up and down to agitate the laundry in the cauldron. Finally, the steaming pieces were transferred from the cauldron with a long wooden paddle, and each piece of soapy laundry was laid on a big wooden table where it was scrubbed with a brush. This procedure not only took time, but also lots of elbow grease.

Water was everywhere, but, fortunately, a grate made of strong wooden boards was on the floor in front of the scrubbing table. The grate meant one did not have to stand on the cold, wet cement floor, which tilted slightly toward a floor drain.

Once the white wash was scrubbed, the colored clothes were taken through the same process, except they were not boiled.

After being scrubbed, the clothes were rinsed in big tubs with cold water, then wrung out by hand and carried outside to dry on the clothesline. Whites that needed bleaching were laid out on the grass and sprinkled with water to bleach.

Because washday was always such a busy and tiring day, we always had a simple meat and vegetable stew that simmered on the stove while Mama was busy with the laundry.

At the end of the basement hall was the door to the storage room. Along one wall, there were shelves for storing apples, quinces, and other fruits. Jars of jellies and jams, canned applesauce, quince sauce, pickles, and vegetables also lined the shelves.

One corner of the room was sectioned off with a board where carrots were kept crisp, layered in sand. I always liked the cool earthy smell of this room. Eggs were kept here during the winter, submerged in *Wasserglas*, a soluble alkaline silicate. The *Wasserglas* sealed the shells to keep bacteria out.

The outside of our house had its special features as well. Having lived in an apartment, my parents loved to spend all the time they could landscaping and making flower and vegetable beds in our yard.

Papa came home every day after work, put on his gardening clothes, took off his dress arm and replaced it with his work prosthesis. Then he and Mama worked outside. Often, it was dark before they allowed themselves to quit.

As customary, the whole property was enclosed with a wooden fence painted white. Along the back fence, a double row of fir trees provided a wind break and privacy. In one corner of the yard, a hole had been dug for compost. Nearby was a raspberry patch where I loved to munch on the best raspberries in the summer. On the two back corners of the house, rain water was collected in large barrels and used to water the flowers and vegetables.

Over the double-wide entrance in front of the property, my parents installed an arbor with climbing roses. The double gate was to accommodate the car Papa was saving for. Because of his war injuries, Papa was not able to drive himself. His dream was for Ludwig to take the family on Sunday outings as soon as he was old enough to drive. No one could have imagined how long Papa would have to hold on to that dream.

Within a few years, my parents had planted both sides of a yard-wide area flanking the wide main drive with rosebushes, daffodil, tulips, carnations, and various perennials, among them lily of the valley, Mama's favorite flower.

Beyond the flower border on the left side of the drive, they laid out a vegetable garden and on the right side an orchard of fruit trees. My parents let me have a tiny plot of my own next to a quince tree. This kept me busy and allowed them to work.

That first fall at the new house, I was helping my parents dig the potatoes. Papa used a sharp three-pronged potato hoe to dig the potatoes, while Mama and I picked them up and put them in a basket. When Papa laid the hoe down to carry the dead potato plants to the compost heap behind the house, I picked up the hoe like I had seen Papa do, lifted it high above my head and swung it down right into my foot. My parents cleaned out the wound with iodine, the only disinfectant available, while I was screaming at the top of my lungs. I still carry the scar today.

I never wanted to help with the potato harvest again. However, the war years would have other plans for me.

I have a great many fond memories associated with growing up in the new house. I remember playing in the yard where Papa, to my delight and also that of the neighborhood kids, had built a *Schiffschaukel,* a swing in the shape of a ship, and a *Turnstange,* horizontal bar.

My cousin Mariele, who was visiting from America,
and I sit with our dolls in the *Schiffschaukel*
that my father built.

When Papa came home one day with a puppy, a Wolfspitz he called it, my joy was complete. To this day, I don't know if there really is such a breed or if he just made up the name to satisfy my curiosity. We named him Lumpi, little vagabond. Since Ludwig was in school and gone a lot, Lumpi became my dog, my constant companion, and my confidant.

I still recall our Sunday outings early every May or June to the ladybug forest, which was a special treat. After paying a fee, we were allowed to enter a fenced-in area of the forest. Big, foil-decorated, chocolate ladybugs with brown legs and antennae covered the trunks of the huge fir trees. It wasn't always easy deciding exactly which one to pick. Sometimes my choice was not within reach of my little hands, so Papa had to lift me up to get my prize. But, oh, how exciting it was to finally get one and take it home. I remember keeping the pretty foil wrapper long after I succumbed to temptation and had eaten the chocolate inside.

In my mind's eye, I see Mama on rainy days, while shelling peas or knitting socks for Papa, telling us stories of her youth, when she and her sister, Marie, played roles in a *Bauernbühne*, folk theater, or when she worked for nobility. Sometimes, she would tell us spooky stories. Amazed and wide-eyed, the neighborhood kids and I would cling to every word she said. Mama was an excellent storyteller.

The house also echoed with the proverbs that Mama and Papa used liberally to guide our lives. If I reached for a sharp object when I was little, Mama would say: "*Messer, Gabel, Scher' und Licht, passt für kleine Kinder nicht*"—knife, fork, scissors and light (matches) are not suited for small children. Should Ludwig or I be slow in getting our homework or chores done, we were reminded with: "*Morgen, morgen, nur nicht heute, sagen alle faulen Leute*"—tomorrow, tomorrow, just not today, that's what all the lazy people say. Pleading to buy some little trinket by saying "it only costs a few pennies," we were reminded that "*Wer den Pfennig nicht ehrt, ist des Taler's nicht wert*"—he who does not honor the penny is not worthy of the dollar.

Papa was a man of few words. If we talked too much at the dinner table, he was quick to tell us: "*Beim Fressen pfeift der Vogel nicht*"—while eating, the bird doesn't sing. "*Viele Hände machen bald ein Ende*"—many hands soon make an end to work—told us to pitch in and help with whatever needed to be done.

To emphasize the importance of learning, Mama told us over and over again, *"Was du hast, kannst du verlieren, aber was du im Kopf hast kann dir niemand nehmen"*—you can lose everything you own, but what you have in your head no one can take from you.

Love and affection were not openly demonstrated, not even in the privacy of one's home. I don't remember ever seeing my parents or the parents of my friends kiss each other. Nevertheless, we felt secure and loved, and we were happy in the shelter of our new house.

Some of my relatives posed with us for this picture in 1933 when my cousin Mariele and her family were visiting from America. From left, front row: Julie, my godmother; Mariele, my cousin; me. From left, back row: Aunt Martha, Julie's mother; Papa; Aunt Marie, Mariele's mother; Aunt Therese; Uncle Georg; and Mama.

From my childhood in Germany, I remember having *Gesundheitskuchen* on Sunday morning. My Aunt Katherine converted my mother's recipe to English measurements and substituted shortening (which we did not have in Germany at that time) for the lard in my mother's recipe. I have often wondered why it is called "health cake."

"Health" Cake—*Gesundheitskuchen*

1 stick butter or margarine
½ c. vegetable shortening
1 ¾ cups sugar
4 eggs
2 ½ cups sifted flour, mixed with 2 teaspoons baking powder
1 cup milk
1 lemon, grated and juiced

Preheat oven to 350 F. Grease and flour a *"Gugelhupf,"* or bundt cake pan.

Cream butter, shortening, and sugar. Add eggs, one at a time, cream well. Add grated lemon zest and juice. Gradually add flour mixture, alternating with milk. Mix in just enough to have a smooth batter. Pour in cake pan and bake at 350 F for 55 to 60 minutes.

Chapter 5

The Christkindlmarkt

The Christmas season in Germany begins with Advent and an outdoor *Christkindlmarkt*, Christmas market, which is held in the larger towns and cities.

To be ready for the first Advent Sunday, we cut and tied fir branches into a wreath and wrapped them with wide red ribbons. Adorned with four fat red candles, the wreath was suspended from the chandelier in the living room. The smell of the fir branches permeated the room as we lit a new candle and sang Christmas songs on each of the next four Sundays. Stollen or Christmas cookies made our Advent Sunday afternoon coffee special.

Each year we eagerly awaited the day when we would go to the *Christkindlmarkt*. Munich's *Marienplatz*, St. Mary's Square, was full of wooden stalls where vendors displayed beautiful hand-blown glass ornaments and brightly painted wooden nutcrackers from the Erz (Ore) Mountains. Christmas pyramids of all sizes explained the story of the Nativity. The pyramids were built so that the heat rising from burning candles on the pyramid's lower tier caused the propeller on top to turn and the figures on the various tiers to move. Advent wreaths, bright shiny stars, treetop angels, colorful toys, and everything else that might be remotely associated with the Christmas season were available there. Perhaps one of the most admired items was the Nativities.

I remember my first visit to the *Christkindlmarkt* and the anticipation I felt beforehand.

"When do we get to go to the *Christkindlmarkt*?" I asked my mother. I had heard from my brother Ludwig about the annual event and was anxious to see it myself.

"Tomorrow is Papa's Saturday off, and we will all go," Mama patiently replied. This was not the first time I'd asked that question.

The next morning I awakened a little earlier than usual. The bathroom was much too cold during this time of the year; it was heated only for the family's weekly baths. So I went into the kitchen where I knew Mama would have a basin filled with warm water on the sink for me to wash up.

After I was dressed, we sat down at the kitchen table to eat breakfast. My place was beside Ludwig on the corner bench. Mama spread a hard roll with butter and jam and poured me a cup of tea, while Ludwig drank milk and my parents had their morning coffee. I could hardly eat I was so excited. Finally, the breakfast dishes were taken care of, and it was time to head to the train station for the short ride to Munich.

As we walked toward the *Marienplatz*, we could already smell the wonderful aroma of sausages being grilled, spiced hot wine, sugar-roasted almonds, and hot chestnuts roasting on big kettle grills.

"Hot chestnuts, come and get a bag . . . hot chestnuts," the vendors shouted as they hawked their wares.

Papa had taken me on his shoulder so that I could see the displays. Munching on hot chestnuts, we were strolling through the crowds, when Mama announced: "Today we'll buy the figurines for the Nativity that Ludwig is building in Papa's workshop."

"I'm finished with the stable, a tripod for the shepherd's cooking fire, and a well with a bucket to haul up the water . . . . I just have to hook up the batteries for light," Ludwig proudly explained.

Turning to Mama, Papa added, "And I'm afraid one of your thimbles is the bucket for the well."

"It was just the right size. All I had to do was to drill two little holes and add a wire handle. It looks good," Ludwig rationalized.

"I want to pick out Baby Jesus and the sheep, can I?" I was quick to ask. "Now we get to have a Nativity, like they have at church."

"Well, it's quite a bit smaller than the one at church . . . . It has to fit on the desk in the living room," Ludwig pointed out.

Moving along the stalls, we soon found figurines that were the right size for the stable. I picked out a baby Jesus in a manger, a shepherd with a lamb over his shoulder and several shepherds standing and lying, and then grazing sheep. Ludwig found three regal looking kings, and to carry their gifts, a camel and a majestic looking elephant, an essential part of a European Nativity.

This is the Nativity that my brother,
Ludwig, built in the 1930s.

"In religion class in school, we learned that St. Francis of Assisi held the first Christmas service in 1223, and he used real people to display a live Nativity," commented Ludwig.

After all of the figurines had been selected, I was allowed to pick out an Advent calendar with twenty-four little doors. One to be opened every day until Christmas Eve.

"Now you can tell just how many days it is until Christmas Eve," Mama pointed out. "You won't have to ask me quite as often."

"But before Christmas, on December 6th, comes Saint Nikolaus. He'll leave us a plate full of nuts, oranges, apples, and cookies. Maybe even a chocolate Saint Nikolaus, if we've been good," Ludwig explained, hope edging his voice.

"Yes, and for bad kids, *Knecht Rupprecht* comes along. He'll rattle his heavy chains and bring coal and switches," admonished Papa. "So, just how good have you two been?"

Ludwig and I just looked at each other and then almost in unison we answered, "Pretty good."

Happy with our treasures, we left the crowd of holiday shoppers behind and headed for home.

Memories of *Sankt Nikolaus Tag*—Saint Nikolaus Day

December 6th is Saint Nikolaus Day. In Bavaria, St. Nikolaus comes with his helper, *Knecht Rupprecht*.

St. Nikolaus, dressed in beautiful bishop's robes with a mitered hat and a staff in his hand, brings a colorful Christmas plate with apples, oranges, cookies, nuts, and a chocolate St. Nikolaus image to good children. He usually leaves his gifts by the front door. His helper, *Knecht Rupprecht,* rattles his chains and leaves switches and coal for bad children. He was also known to take very bad children away in his gunny sack.

Needless to say, my conscience was not always clear. While I didn't think I had been bad enough to be taken away in the gunny sack by *Knecht Rupprecht,* I sometimes thought it best to hide behind the davenport, thinking that would prevent me from getting switches. Luckily, I never got switches or coal but always a big plate with treats of a chocolate St. Nikolaus, cookies, *Lebkuchen,* which looked very much like the ones Mama baked, mandarin oranges, figs, and nuts.

One icy St. Nikolaus Day, the chocolate St. Nikolaus on my plate was broken. Mama explained that St. Nikolaus must have slipped on the ice. Mama had a sore knee for several days, but I didn't make the connection. I was a believer.

Chapter 6

A Special Holiday Season

Christmas Eve finally arrived, with a sprinkling of snow and a flurry of activity.

Papa's niece, Fanny, had come several weeks earlier to help. Mama and Fanny had been cleaning house and doing the Christmas baking. The aroma of spices and fruits soaked in rum permeated the air.

Stollen, a yeast cake studded with slivered almonds and candied fruit, *Lebkuchen, Haselnußlaiberl*, hazelnut cookies, *Anislaiberl*, anis cookies, and *Spitzbuben*, a rich butter cookie, had been baked, carefully packaged and put in the storeroom to keep cool and dry. The *Kletzenbrot*, a loaf of dried fruits moistened with rum, wrapped in dough and baked, was also aging there.

There was an air of secrecy and lots of private whispering going on. The living room had been locked for several days so that the *Christkindl*, Christ child, would not be disturbed while bringing the Christmas tree and presents. In Bavaria, the Christ child is the bringer of gifts and is depicted as an angel.

Now it was time to get ready for dinner and the festivities. Earlier, Papa had lighted the wood fire in the firebox under the hammered brass water reservoir in the bathroom to heat the water and to get the room warm. Mama bathed me, then gave me my favorite tub toys.

"You can play in the tub while I quickly run to the store. Fanny will come and check on you," Mama instructed while she allowed some of the water to drain out.

"But what if the *Christkindl* comes?" I objected.

"Well, when *Christkindl* rings the bell, we can go see what He has brought. If we go too soon, we'll scare the *Christkindl* away. Fanny or I will get you long before that," Mama assured me.

Mama left for the store while Fanny set the table and watched over the various dishes that were bubbling on the wood-burning stove.

It was always fun to play in the warm water, but tonight I was far too excited. I really wanted to be downstairs. Picking up my little green frog I wondered what was going on downstairs. *Will Fanny remember to get me?* I chased the frog with the big fish. *Did I hear a door downstairs? . . . Maybe that's Mama coming back . . . now they'll get me.* I picked up the frog and started to play, then threw him to the end of the tub. *I don't want to play anymore . . . .*

I couldn't wait any longer. Getting out of the tub, dripping wet, without a stitch of clothing, I went out into the cold hallway and started down the curved stairway. Halfway down the stairs, I could see light through the transom window of the living room door. *There is light in the living room . . . the Christkindl came, and I didn't even hear Christkindl's bell . . . .*

Papa and Ludwig were still finishing the arrangement of the last few figurines of the Nativity. When I opened the door, they looked like they had been caught red-handed at some crime, but I only noticed the beautiful Christmas tree which touched the ceiling.

"Ah, the *Christkindl* came," I announced jubilantly and then protested: "Mama promised to get me, and she didn't, nobody did," my teeth chattering with cold.

"Mama's still at the store, and you're supposed to be upstairs. Just look at you . . . no clothes and dripping wet," Papa growled as he picked me up and whisked me into the kitchen, unceremoniously dumping me into Fanny's arms. "Here, you better get her dressed."

Fanny briskly dried and dressed me, all the while admonishing me that I could have caught my death of a cold or even pneumonia. But I didn't hear any of it. All I had on my mind was that glimpse of the tree and the table with the presents.

We had our usual Christmas Eve meal of various kinds of hot sausages, several salads, and breads. It was hard to concentrate on the mealtime prayer and eating, but finally we were done. Papa had left the kitchen, Fanny was clearing the table while Mama was taking off my apron and washing my hands and face, when we heard the soft tinkling of a little bell.

I rushed into the living room to see the Christmas tree aglow with red wax candles and the Nativity with the shepherd's fire burning. The star above the stable was illuminating it all. Standing in front of the tree, I recited the short poem that Fanny had taught me. Ludwig played "*Stille Nacht*" ("Silent Night") and "*O, Tannenbaum*" on the piano, and then it was time for the *Bescherung*, the opening of the gifts.

Spread out on the table were presents for everyone. As was the custom, the presents were not wrapped. Instead, they were adorned with festive-looking pine branches and bright red ribbons. There was a "*Max und Moritz*" book, a new dress, stockings, and a doll for me. Ludwig received the book "*Winnetou*" from the popular series by Karl May, some new clothes, and several accessories for his train set.

There was also a package from Aunt Katherine in America with presents for all of us. For me, she had sent brightly colored hard candy, a kaleidoscope, and a box of crayons. Crayons were unknown in Germany, and I found it much easier to color with them than with the colored pencils we used. The kaleidoscope fascinated me with all the changing and shifting colors and shapes. Unfortunately, I was so curious about what made all of these shapes, that a few weeks later I couldn't stand the suspense any longer. I wanted to see the wondrous things inside and carefully opened it. It was quite a disappointment to find that only bits and pieces of colored glass had created this wonderful illusion.

Along with the package there was also a Christmas card showing a living room scene with a fire in the fireplace and children with their Christmas stockings.

"Look, Mama, there's a fire in the living room. Won't their house burn down?"

I questioned. "And why are they drying socks by that fire?"

"That is an open fireplace, and children hang their stockings there to get small presents."

"I want to visit Aunt Katherine and Uncle Joe and my cousin Joey. Can we?" I pleaded.

"No, America is much too far away. It takes a ship many days to get across the ocean to America . . . ."

"When I get big, I'm going to America and visit Aunt Katherine and my cousin Joey."

"Well, we do have a few years before that happens. Now I'm going to cut some *Stollen* and fix us some *Glühwein,* warm spiced wine, and we'll sing Christmas carols."

Soon Ludwig was at the piano, and everyone was gathered around to sing Christmas carols. Everyone except me. I was busy marching the sheep toward the stable for baby Jesus.

"Anneliese! You know better than that. The Nativity figurines are not toys to be played with . . . Just look at this lamb. It has a broken leg." Mama scolded.

"It was a present for baby Jesus. I was just helping it to get there," I replied in my own defense, and questioned: "Can you fix it, Papa?"

"I'll see what I can do tomorrow," Papa promised.

Later, we walked through the quiet, starry night to attend Midnight Mass. With every step, the snow crunched under our feet.

On the next day, Christmas Day, we had a feast of the traditional Christmas goose, potato dumplings to soak up the rich gravy, red cabbage, a potato salad with curly endive added, and a celeriac salad. This was followed at four o'clock with coffee and *Torte,* a rich multilayered cake.

On December 26, also a legal holiday in Germany, Uncle Georg and Aunt Therese, as well as Aunt Martha and my godmother, Julie, stopped by in the afternoon for coffee, *Stollen* and Christmas goodies.

Julie gave me a *Sammeltasse,* a pretty china cup with a saucer and dessert plate in a beautiful pattern. The cup was filled with chocolates, and the whole thing was wrapped in cellophane and tied with a bright red ribbon. While the candy was for my immediate gratification, the cup set was put away to be part of my trousseau for when I married. It was assumed that girls would get married. By the time I was ready to marry, I could host an afternoon coffee with every guest having a different china place setting.

When I was older, Mama invited Herr Kammermeier, Ludwig's and my piano teacher, as well as some of our relatives for refreshments on December 26th. Mama served cookies, coffee and also *Käsestangen,* or cheese sticks, and the black currant liqueur she had made with the black currants from our garden.

Herr Kammermeier always helped himself to plenty of the refreshments, but he was certainly not one of my favorite people. During my piano lessons, he sat next to me, and if I had not practiced as much as he thought I should have, he pulled the hair above my ear saying: "*Wir haben wieder 'mal nicht genügend geübt,*" we haven't practiced enough again.

At Mama's coffee, while helping himself to plenty of the cheese sticks and liqueur, Herr Kammermeier never failed to extol Ludwig's progress, while Anneliese, in his opinion, was a different matter. He obviously had not figured out that since Ludwig did so well (he was now also playing with the concert orchestra at the *Gymnasium*), I had decided that piano was not going to be worthy of my efforts. I liked hearing Ludwig play the piano and was proud of my big brother, but I thought I could never come up to that level of perfection. If I was to excel at something, it certainly was not the piano. I finally persuaded my parents to let me play the flute instead. That was the end of Herr Kammermeier for me.

New Year's Eve, after supper, our neighbors, Herr and Frau Soller, came to help us see in the New Year. Herr Soller, a short, stocky fellow, brought along his accordion, and we all sang Christmas songs and some songs from the Rhineland area where Herr Soller had spent his youth. He also was a good story teller and entertained us with some fascinating stories.

After the singing, Mama got things ready for the Bavarian custom of lead pouring. Lead was melted and then everyone took a small dipper, filled it with the melted lead, and poured it into a pan of very cold water. The shape the lead took in the cold water supposedly forecast one's future. As we each took a turn, much laughter was heard as we tried to interpret what the future would have in store for us. With Mama's help, I was allowed to pour a dipper. It came out in the form of a stick with a hat on it.

"Hey, Maugei, you're going far, far away," Ludwig prophesied, calling me by the nickname he had for me.

"Well, I hope not," Mama protested. "We'd all miss her terribly."

Mama then brought in refreshments. To close the end of the year, we toasted the new year with *Glühwein,* hot spiced wine, wishing each other good luck, good health, and good fortune. I loved to hear my little glass clink with everyone else's glasses. Finally, after midnight, everyone went upstairs to the attic windows to "ooh" and "ahh" at the spectacular fireworks display in Munich.

On New Year's Day, I followed my parents around as they burned incense and used chalk to write the letters K + M + B, the initials of the three holy kings—Kaspar, Melchior, and Balthasar—on the top part of each door in our house. This was to ensure blessings for the house and its inhabitants for the year that had just begun.

The holiday season was so busy that Mama usually didn't send Christmas cards but New Year's cards instead. It was appropriate to send these at any time during the month of January. The cards had various good wishes for a happy, healthy year to come and good luck symbols, such as a four-leaf clover, a horseshoe, a little pig, a toadstool mushroom, or a chimney sweep, but never a rabbit's foot. Unlike in America, a rabbit's foot is not a good luck symbol in Germany.

This special holiday season that had started with Advent, the *Christkindlmarkt* and the coming of St. Nikolaus was over, but the memories it created are still with me today.

Oma Heider's *Lebkuchen*

3 cups flour
1/2 teaspoons baking soda
1/2 teaspoon salt
1 teaspoon allspice
1 teaspoon nutmeg
1 teaspoon cinnamon
1 teaspoon cloves
3/4 cup brown sugar
1 egg
1 cup honey
1 tablespoon fresh lemon juice
2 teaspoons freshly grated lemon peel
1/2 cup chopped walnuts
1-1/2 cups chopped candied fruit

Warm honey. Add sugar, lemon juice and peel. Beat in egg and dry ingredients. Stir in candied fruit and nuts. Chill overnight.

Preheat oven to 350 F. Roll out dough (not too thin) on floured surface. Cut with round cookie cutter. Bake on greased cookie sheet for about 12 minutes. Do not let get brown.

Make a thin icing of powdered sugar, water, and fresh lemon juice. Brush on cookies while barely warm.

Lebkuchen will keep in tins for weeks. A small slice of apple added to the tin will keep cookies soft.

Spitzbuben—Jam-Filled Cookies

2 cups butter, room temperature
1 cup sugar
4 egg yolks
2 teaspoons freshly grated lemon rind
2 teaspoons vanilla
1/2 teaspoon salt
5-1/3 cups sifted flour
Seedless red raspberry jam
Powdered sugar

Cream butter and sugar. Add the egg yolks, one at a time. Add lemon rind and vanilla and beat well. Add about 4 cups of the flour and knead in the rest of the flour. Wrap dough in plastic wrap and chill 1 hour.

Preheat oven to 375 F. On pastry cloth, roll out dough to 1/4-inch thickness. Cut out cookies with a round or star-shaped cookie cutter. With a small round cutter (or a thimble), cut a hole in half of the cookie rounds.

Bake on ungreased cookie sheet for about 12 minutes. Do not let cookies get brown.

Cool. Spread cookies with raspberry jam and cover with the cookies that have a hole in center. Sprinkle with powdered sugar.

Rotkohl—Red Cabbage

In Bavaria, where I come from, we call red cabbage *Blaukraut,* or blue cabbage, not *Rotkohl.*

3 slices bacon, cut in strips
1 medium onion, chopped
1 tart apple, peeled, cored, and chopped
1 head red cabbage, finely shredded
1 tablespoon sugar
4 tablespoons vinegar
Small glass red wine (optional)
Beef broth, as needed
1 teaspoon salt and pepper, to taste

In a large saucepan, brown the bacon and set aside. Drain off most of the bacon grease. In a small amount of bacon grease*, sauté the onion until it is glassy. Add cabbage, apples, sugar, vinegar, wine, and beef broth. Stir to mix ingredients and simmer, uncovered, for 15 minutes. Cover pan and simmer 20 minutes more or until cabbage is tender. Stir occasionally. Correct seasoning.

*A small amount of vegetable oil may be used instead of bacon grease.
Note: This can be made the day before. Some say it tastes even better reheated.

Later Christmas Memories

Ludwig and I did not get many presents at Christmas. Sometimes there was a little crocheted doll blanket or some clothing Mama had made for my doll. Usually, we received some new items of clothing and perhaps a toy or a game. We could always count on getting a new book. The presents were arranged on the table, never wrapped.

One year, I received a beautiful doll with blond curls, a soft body, and porcelain hands and feet. When it was my bedtime, I wanted to take my new doll to bed with me like I did Teddy. Mama, however, told me that I'd better let dolly sit in the chair beside my bed so she would not fall out of bed and break.

One night a month or two later, feeling lonely, I pulled dolly into bed with me only to wake up the next morning to find several small porcelain fingers in bed with me. Until next Christmas, my doll had several fingers missing. The following Christmas Eve I found my doll, with new hands, in her little carriage beside the Christmas tree. I was told the *Christkindl* had taken her to the doll hospital. I had learned my lesson. Dolly slept in her carriage or on the chair beside my bed from then on.

When I was a little older, my Christmas present was a *Kaufladen*, a toy grocery store about the size of a doll house. Complete with a counter, it had three rows of drawers and a battery-powered bell for my customers to ring. It was stocked with chocolate coffee beans, candies in the shape of green peas, *marzipan* potatoes, almond paste formed into potatoes and rolled in cocoa, various fruits and vegetables made of marzipan, and even marzipan hams and sausages.

On the counter, there was a small scale to weigh things and a supply of little paper bags. All I needed was customers. Ludwig was quick to volunteer, and he promised to return the items he purchased. To my dismay, he often not only ate the goodies but also the gold-foil-wrapped, chocolate money.

After I learned how to read, I put *Grimm's Märchen* on my wish list. I had seen this beautifully illustrated book of fairy tales when Mama and I had been shopping in Munich. Now it was Advent but still so many days until Christmas Eve. I was impatient. Would I get my book?

The last time Mama had been in Munich I was in school. Did she buy the book then?

I could not wait.

Mama was out grocery shopping, and I decided to look around. I knew Mama put *Poohl's Flieder Seife,* her favorite lilac-scented soap, and other little treasures in the linen closet. I decided to look there, and that is where I finally found the book, nestled in among the pillow cases.

I started to put it back carefully, when I decided to read just one short story. I had not yet finished the story when I heard the garden gate close. It was Mama returning home. I quickly made the tiniest pencil mark where I had stopped reading and put the book back in its hiding place. I was happy. I had found the book, and I would get it Christmas Eve.

However, temptation was too much, and the next time and every time Mama went shopping I read more. I actually read quite a few stories that way.

Christmas Eve came, and I was astonished. I didn't see "my book" on the gift table. Feeling guilty, I didn't say anything. Neither did my parents. A few days later, the suspense was too much for me, and I asked Mama about the book.

"Mama, I thought maybe I'd get the book for Christmas, you know the *Grimm's Fairy Tales* we saw in Munich."

"Well, you know I was very disappointed to find pencil marks in the book. I didn't want to give you a used book. Do you have any idea what happened?"

I felt terrible that I had disappointed Mama. As much as I hated to do it, I confessed to what I had done. I finally got the book; I believe it was not until my birthday in February.

Mama's *Johannisbeerlikör*—Black Currant Liqueur

My mother made this sweet liqueur ever since I can remember. She would serve it after special afternoon coffees or after dinner.

1,000 grams (2 pounds plus 1 cup) black currants, washed, stemmed, and put into a strainer to dry
6 to 8 whole allspice
1 liter (4-1/4 cups) 90 to 95 percent alcohol (I use Everclear)
2 liters water (8-1/2 cups)
1,500 grams sugar (7-1/2 cups)

1. Place currants and the whole allspice into a one-gallon, wide-mouth jar or non-metal container, and pour the alcohol over them. Put on a lid and let stand in a sunny window (or on a sunny porch) for four to six weeks.
2. After four to six weeks, boil the water and sugar until the sugar is dissolved. Pour the water-sugar syrup into the berry and alcohol mixture. Put back into jar with lid and let stand in a sunny window for another four weeks.
3. Strain the mixture through a cheesecloth-lined sieve, then pour the liqueur into sterilized bottles.

This can be enjoyed as a liqueur or mixed with sparkling water, champagne, or white or red wine.

Mama's *Käsestangen*—Caraway Cheese Sticks

120 grams (1 cup) flour
120 grams (1 ½ cups) grated Emmenthaler cheese*
100 grams (7 tablespoons) butter
1 egg yolk, lightly beaten with 1 teaspoon water
Caraway seeds

Blend all ingredients in Cuisinart. Chill.
Preheat oven to 350 F.
On pastry cloth, roll out dough to a thickness of about one-fourth inch. Cut into strips about 4-1/2 inches long and 1/2-inch wide. Brush with beaten egg yolk and sprinkle with caraway seeds.

Bake on ungreased baking sheet until golden, about 10 to 12 minutes.

* Can substitute any freshly grated hard cheese such as Asiago or Parmesan.

Chapter 7

The Masked Ball

It was February and the customary pre-Lenten carnival parades and balls with the revelers in elaborate costumes were in full swing.

Fasching, as it is called in Bavaria, is primarily observed in the Catholic regions of Germany and also is known as *Fastnacht* or *Karnival*. But whatever its name, it includes not only adults but children as well.

One of the old customs Mama told me about concerns the market wives from the *Viktualien* and *Rindermarkt*, the two big outdoor markets in Munich. On Shrove Tuesday, the day before Ash Wednesday, women proceed to the big fountain on the *Marienplatz*. Once there, they take off the large leather money purses they wear around their waists and wash them in the fountain, then turn them inside out to show that they are empty, implying that all of their money has been spent during the frivolity and gaiety of the *Faschings* season.

On the outskirts of Munich where we lived, one of the big events was the children's annual masked ball that was held at the Restaurant Spitzauer. This was my first ball, and Mama was getting me dressed as Little Red Riding Hood. Ludwig was ready in his polka dot clown costume with a stiffly starched neck ruffle, a pointed hat on his head. Mama wore a fantasy costume with a tight-fitting bodice and a bouffant skirt. Her dark auburn hair was parted in the middle with long curls on each side and flowers framing her face.

"You look so pretty, Mama," I said, hugging her.

"And so do you," was Mama's reply. "We better hurry and finish getting you dressed."

Mama and Ludwig pose together
at the annual pre-Lenten Children's Ball.

I'm the one in the front row (far right).
I'm three years old, dressed as Little Red Riding Hood,
at my first Children's Ball.

The big ballroom was alive with colorfully dressed masqueraders of all kinds. Balancing heavy trays of food and beverages, waiters and waitresses carefully made their way through the crowd. We occupied an empty table and also saved a seat for Papa, who would join us after work.

When the dance floor was cleared, two of the masqueraders stepped onto it and began dancing to the minuet the orchestra was playing. They were dressed as a courtier and his lady, associated with the time of the French queen Marie-Antoinette.

Atop the gentleman's powdered white wig was a black tri-cornered hat that matched his dark jacket. A ruffled shirt, satin knee trousers, hose, and shoes with big silver buckles completed his costume. The lady's exquisite gown was of ivory satin and lace with side hoops. She also had on a white wig, and two long corkscrew curls framed her face, which was accented by a black beauty spot. A saucy, plumed hat was perched on her head. She carried a fan, which she used in a flirtatious manner as she and her partner curtsied and bowed to the music.

I was fascinated. *It must have been just like this when Mama was one of the cooks on the staff of Count Wrede.* Mama had often told me of the elegant dinners, the formal teas and the festive balls they had to cook for. She had described the nobility that attended these gala affairs in their fine clothing and glittering jewelry, and their arrival in stately carriages. I could visualize the handsome men and the beautiful ladies who long ago would have bowed and danced late into the night.

"Mama, I want to dance like that lady and man. Can you teach me?" I begged.

"Those are the two Biedermeier sisters. The older sister is simply dressed as a man," Mama explained. "The minuet is an old dance. I don't know how to dance it. But when you're a little older, you can go to dance classes that are held for girls and boys. There you will learn how to dance and how to behave at dances."

"How long do I have to wait? I want to do it now!" was my impatient plea.

"Well, let's start today. Papa and I can teach you some dance steps."

The couple had finished their performance to great applause from the audience. The orchestra struck up a new tune and soon the dance floor was filled with children and parents.

Papa had joined us. Now the whole family was on the dance floor. Mama was dancing with Ludwig, who was doing quite well, having attended several of these balls in the past. Papa had picked me up and was dancing around with me on his arm. I squealed with delight. Then, putting me down, he tried some simple steps with me, one, two, three, turn . . . .

The dancing left us famished, so back at our table, we ordered hot sausages, potato salad, rolls, and beverages. I was allowed to have more apple juice, a drink I dearly loved. The evening sped by quickly, and, before we knew it, the ball was over.

My first ball had been a wonderful, magical evening. I could not get the graceful dancers, the kaleidoscopic costumes, and the graceful minuet out of my mind. It was a short walk home, but I seemed to be floating on air all of the way.

Chapter 8

Special Holidays and a Visit to the Circus

The Christmas season, the children's ball, my birthday, and going to the circus were definitely the highlights of the winter for me, but other holidays throughout the year also played a special role in our family.

Whenever family name days, or birthdays, came around, we would be busy for days ahead making cards and small gifts. Mother's Day was no exception. We always diligently made our own cards. Going to the store to buy a card was out of the question since we had no allowance, and one really could not ask one's mother for money to buy her own card.

Usually, we asked Papa for money to buy Mama a small gift. I remember buying her a box of her favorite soap, some cologne, or a book Aunt Therese had recommended. Papa gave Ludwig the money, and Ludwig and I would go and buy the gift.

I always felt that we also had to have flowers. What would Mother's Day be without flowers? Flowers from our garden, from the flower beds that she had tended, would not do. They already belonged to her. The only acceptable answer was to get the flowers from someone else's garden.

I usually waited until after the evening meal and then "went out to play." There were always plenty of lilacs or snowballs that hung over the fence, just waiting for my friends and me to pick them. It was great if an early peony or some other flower peeked through the fence, beckoning us to add it to our bouquet.

At home, I stored my flowers in a bucket in the basement or garage until the next morning when I proudly presented these flowers, along with my homemade card and our gift, to Mama.

My birthday was always special. It was my day, and I felt like I was queen for a day. On the Sunday afternoon before my birthday, Uncle Georg, Aunt Therese, my godmother, Julie, and her mother, Aunt Martha, came to join us for birthday cake and coffee. Uncle Georg and Aunt Therese always brought me an eagerly anticipated book, while I received a *Sammeltasse*, a china dessert plate, saucer, and cup filled with chocolates, from my godmother Julie and a small gift from Aunt Martha. I always eagerly awaited this family get-together for my birthday, not only for the presents but for the warm feeling that being in their midst created.

About a week before my birthday, Mama asked what I would like for my birthday dinner. My menu didn't vary much from year to year. I always asked for *Griessnockerlsuppe,* farina dumplings in chicken broth, *Kalbsnierenbraten,* rolled kidney veal roast, *Semmelknödel,* bread dumplings, gravy, potato and cucumber salad, and lettuce salad.

For my birthday cake, Mama made my favorite cake, a hedgehog cake. Layers of ladyfingers were cut to create the form of a hedgehog. Coffee-flavored butter cream covered each layer and also frosted the assembled cake. Toasted slivered almonds were stuck in the frosting to resemble the quills. Last of all, raisins were added for the eyes and nose.

There were no elaborate birthday presents. My brother, Ludwig, usually gave me a chocolate bar or a few chocolates. From my parents, I often received a game, a book, and a special item of clothing. A very special present from Papa always was tickets for the family to go to the circus at a later date. While I almost knew Papa would bring these tickets, I always eagerly awaited the moment he would reach into his pocket and pull out the magical tickets.

Circus Krone, Europe's largest circus, had its winter headquarters in Munich. The rest of the year would find it traveling all over Europe. Papa had brought home the anticipated tickets and for the last several weeks we had longed for "Circus Day" to arrive. But this year's visit was to end differently. It was to cast a dark shadow over my young life.

Mama awakened me early with hot oatmeal on a tray.

"I put some red raspberry syrup on the oatmeal," Mama coaxed. "Sit up so you can eat it."

I hated oatmeal, and I hated this new ritual of being awakened early, being force-fed oatmeal, and then trying to go back to sleep for another hour before getting up to go to school. Mama had complained to the family doctor that I was unusually pale and thin and that she was worried about me.

So the doctor had prescribed oatmeal along with some putrid-tasting liquid medicine, which was to "put some color in my cheeks and some meat on my bones," as he said. I finally got the oatmeal down, but I was too excited to go back to sleep. Today, we would go to the circus.

The day started out beautifully, a mild day with bright sunshine and scattered white clouds, like fluffy cotton candy. The first hint of spring was in the air. Happy and full of expectation, I skipped home from school, after having told all of my friends that I was going to the circus that evening.

"You don't need to change your school clothes today," Mama informed me as she opened the door. Usually I had to take off my "good clothes" before I could go outside and play.

"You can go ahead and practice your letters on the slate, or read the new words you learned in school today to me."

After an early supper, my parents, Ludwig, and I took the train to Munich and then walked to the Circus Krone building. We found our seats, and I could hardly sit still in anticipation of the performance. It wasn't long until the clowns in their droll costumes and painted faces came somersaulting and tumbling into the arena to entertain the crowd with their pranks while late-comers were being seated.

A blast of trumpets heralded the entrance of the ringmaster. He looked dashing in white jodhpurs and tails complete with top hat. Waving his silver-tipped cane, he welcomed us to the greatest show on earth.

Massive elephants with wrinkled, rough skin entered the arena, trunk to tail, their smooth ears flapping like the sails of a sailboat. Their massive bodies were upheld by feet the size of tree trunks. Atop were pretty ladies, effortlessly directing the gargantuan beasts.

I was enthralled and visualized myself in their place. It had to be truly wonderful to be able to perform in a circus.

The crowd was in awe as a sleek-looking tiger jumped through burning hoops, overcoming his innate fear of fire. This was followed by acrobats from Romania, who performed spectacular feats on the high wire with apparent ease.

Meticulously groomed white horses in dress harness carried ladies in sequined costumes who were executing all kinds of intricate acrobatics in perfect synchronization.

The next act featured a powerful lion that stood on a platform. I held my breath as a white horse ran beneath the platform and the lion jumped onto the horse, riding it around the arena and back to the platform. The lion jumped back onto the platform, and then they repeated this act several more times.

"I think the horse is shaking. It's afraid of the lion, isn't it, Papa?" I whispered.

"The horse has heavy padding on its back, instead of a saddle. That protects it, and they both have been trained for a long time to work together," Papa assured me. The horse exited the arena. A shiver ran down my spine as the trainer confidently placed his head into the lion's mouth, before they, too, left the arena.

I loved watching the animals perform, the tense excitement, the sweet smell of the cotton candy and the burnt almonds, the pungent smell of the arena. Even though it was getting late, I regretted seeing the clowns return to lead in the parade of the performers and animals, signaling the end of the show.

The circus crowd, theater- and movie-goers, as well as people who had worked late, all were hurrying to catch the last train home. The train was packed, and we saw no empty seats. A young man got up and kindly offered Mama his seat, which she gratefully took. Now she was able to hold me on her lap. As I fell asleep to the rhythmic clatter of the train, I could smell the familiar scent of Mama's cologne, Lily of the Valley, her favorite flower.

Ludwig had gone into the next car to find a seat. Getting off the train at our destination, we looked around for Ludwig but didn't see him. Thinking he had probably fallen asleep and was still on the train, Papa told Mama and me to start walking home.

"I'm going to ask the stationmaster to phone ahead and have them send Ludwig back on the returning train," he said. "Then I'll catch up with you."

While we were at the circus, the weather had turned. It was a cloudy, moonless night. I was still half asleep and dragging my feet when Mama and I reached the place where we could either take a shortcut through the now-deserted restaurant beer garden or walk a little farther to our street, with houses on the left side and an open field on the right.

The beer garden had a tall board fence on two sides, making it a very secluded place. Dark, old, horse chestnut trees gave it a sinister and spooky look. Mama did not like to take the shortcut at night, but she considered doing so because she knew I was extremely tired. However, her apprehension prevailed. She could not bring herself to take the shortcut.

Suddenly, out of nowhere, a man on a bicycle cut in front of us, barring the road. His coat collar was turned up, and his hat was pulled down into his face. *He must have been coming from behind the fence of the beer garden. Why? At this late time? The restaurant has been closed for hours . . . .* The stranger tried to engage Mama in a conversation. In a strangely smooth, but urgent, voice, he offered to escort us home, all the while trying to maneuver us toward the shortcut and into the darkened beer garden.

"Leave us alone. My husband is coming at any moment," Mama yelled at the man, grabbing my arm and hand even tighter. Mama turned around, heading back toward the station. The man screeched around on his bicycle and again cut off our way, trying to force us to take the shortcut. Mama now started shouting at the top of her voice:

"Martl, Martl! Help, help!" I had never heard my mother yell this loud. I felt Mama shaking. *What does this man want? Where is Papa? . . . We need you, Papa.*

Suddenly the man threw his bike down and grabbed Mama from behind.

"Papa, Papa! Come help us! Papa, Papa!" I was crying in desperation.

When the man tried to put his hand over Mama's mouth, she bit him, at the same time struggling to get free, and hanging on to me. My hand hurt from her tight grip on me.

The man had dropped his fake manner. He now was cursing and forcing us into the beer garden, when we heard steps from someone running toward us. It was Papa.

Hearing Mama's desperate screams, he knew something was terribly wrong, and he started running as fast as his legs would carry him. With Papa approaching, the stranger let go of Mama, rushed back to his bicycle, jumped on, and quickly disappeared in the opposite direction. Papa picked me up and took hold of Mama's arm and held her tight. Mama was shaking violently and could not stop her tears of relief.

"He's gone. It's OK now. You're safe. Let's get you home." Papa handed Mama his handkerchief.

"I couldn't see his face, but I know that voice. I've heard that voice before, but I don't know where . . . or when," Mama kept sobbing over and over.

"Don't try to figure that out now . . . . Let's go and get Anneliese to bed . . . . We'll deal with the rest tomorrow," Papa said, trying to calm her.

Papa carried me the rest of the way home. Safely at home, Mama made us some chamomile tea, gave me a sip of *Johannisbeerlikör*, the black currant liqueur, and then put me to bed with my teddy bear.

"Mama, why was that man so mean to us? Why didn't he let us go home?"

"That was a sick man. You're safe now. No one can hurt you. Tell me what you liked best about the circus," Mama tried to reassure me, but I interrupted her.

"I'm afraid for Ludwig. I want my brother to come home. I don't want that man to hurt Ludwig."

"That man is gone, and Papa is going back to the station to pick up Ludwig when the train comes back. No one is going to hurt Ludwig, not with Papa around. Now I'll listen to your prayer, and then you can dream about the pretty white horses at the circus and the clowns that made you laugh, OK? I'll sit here by your bed and sing you and Teddy to sleep."

I said the short prayer I had been taught, and Mama sprinkled holy water from the container on the wall on my forehead. Then she started singing softly, *"Schlaf', Kindlein, schlaf', dein Vater hüt' die Schaf'* . . . Sleep, baby, sleep, your father herds the sheep . . . ."

Hard as she tried, my mother could not identify the voice from that harrowing night nor could she overcome her new reluctance to go anywhere alone when it grew dark.

Over a year later, a man was arrested for several rape-murders. Mama now remembered where she had heard the voice of the man on the bike before. It was several years before, when we lived in the apartments. The man and his parents and sisters still lived there. My parents were stunned. He was a quiet young man who was kind of a loner, but he had always greeted my parents politely when they had met him on the street.

The newspaper accounts of the man's arrest and conviction brought back all of the memories of that terrifying night for our family, especially for Mama. We now realized just how timely Papa's arrival had been. Future visits to the circus never were the same happy experiences they had been. There was always the haunting memory of that one dark night.

Grießnockerlsuppe—Cream of Wheat Dumpling Soup

1 cup milk
2 tablespoons butter
3/4 teaspoon salt
6 tablespoons Cream of Wheat
1 lightly beaten egg
Chopped parsley, to taste
Pinch of nutmeg
4 cups chicken broth
Chopped chives (garnish)

Bring milk to a boil. Add butter and salt. While stirring, add the Cream of Wheat. Continue stirring, over low heat until the mass pulls away from the side of the pan and forms a ball. Cool about 10 minutes. Add the egg, parsley, and nutmeg. Let stand for 20 minutes.

Bring chicken broth to a boil. Use 2 teaspoons to form small *Nockerl*, oblong-shaped (or round) dumplings. Drop dumplings into the boiling broth. Simmer for 10 minutes. Sprinkle with chopped chives (or more parsley) and serve. Serves 6 to 8.

Semmelknödel—Bread Dumplings

8 stale hard rolls (I use rolls such as Earth Grains' French style
 or Baker's Dozen)
1 teaspoon salt
1¼ to 1½ cups warm milk*
2 tablespoons butter or margarine
1 medium onion, chopped fine
1 tablespoon chopped parsley
2 tablespoons flour
2 eggs
Bread crumbs, if needed to firm dough

Cut rolls into thin slices and put in large bowl. Sprinkle with salt.
Add 1 tablespoon butter to milk, and heat until melted. Pour over
rolls, and let stand 30 minutes to one hour.

Sauté onion in 1 tablespoon butter until glassy but not brown.
Add onion, parsley, flour, and eggs to rolls and mix thoroughly.

Bring a large pot of water to a boil. Add some salt. Moisten hands
in a bowl of water and form a "test" dumpling. Lower dumpling into
the boiling water. If dumpling keeps its shape and does not fall apart
within a minute or two, add the rest of the dumplings.** Simmer for
20 minutes.

These dumplings are always served with lots of gravy.

* The amount of liquid depends on how dry your bread is.

** If the dumpling falls apart, add dry bread crumbs, a tablespoon
at a time, until the batter is firm enough.

Bayrischer Kartoffelsalat—Bavarian Potato Salad

6 to 8 firm, white, waxy potatoes (not baking potatoes)
1/4 cup finely chopped onion or green onion
3 tablespoons vegetable oil
1 cup water
1 chicken bouillon cube
1/4 cup white wine vinegar
Salt and pepper, to taste
Freshly chopped chives

Wash potatoes and cook in their skin. Peel while still warm and slice thinly into large bowl. Add onion and sprinkle with vegetable oil. In large measuring cup, mix water, bouillon cube, and vinegar. Heat until warm and pour over potatoes. Add salt, pepper, and chives.* Gently mix. Correct seasonings.

Let stand for one-half hour before serving. Sprinkle more chives on top.

* You can mix potato salad with cucumber salad or endive salad at this point.

Kopfsalat—Boston Bibb Lettuce

1 head Boston Bibb lettuce (butter lettuce)
4 tablespoons vegetable oil
2 tablespoons vinegar
Salt, pepper
Fresh chopped chives (optional)

Wash lettuce. Break into bite-sized pieces. Mix oil and vinegar; salt and pepper to taste. Pour over lettuce and toss. Serve immediately.
NOTE: I like to crisp the lettuce by soaking it for 15 minutes in ice water.

Tomatensalat—Tomato Salad

4 sliced tomatoes
2 tablespoons chopped onions, or green onions
Chopped chives
Dressing:
1/2 cup vegetable oil
3 tablespoons vinegar
3/4 teaspoon salt
1 pinch sugar

Arrange sliced tomatoes in a bowl. Sprinkle with chopped onions, and pour the dressing over all. Sprinkle with the chives.

Note: Salad is better if allowed to marinate for an hour or two.

Chapter 9

Early Schooldays

My earliest recollection of school actually doesn't come from my experience but rather from Ludwig's transition from public school to the *Gymnasium*. Ludwig was in fourth grade when his teachers encouraged my parents to send him to the *Gymnasium*. This created such a stir in our family that I became aware of the fact that there was school, and that I, too, would be going to school one of these days.

The *Gymnasium*, a nine-year school, stressed academics and prepared students for study at the university. In order to study at the *Gymnasium*, parents were required to pay a rather steep monthly tuition. Papa was not so sure that this expense was necessary. He felt Ludwig should learn a trade. After all, he had learned a trade, and didn't he provide well for his family?

But Mama was adamant. She had always wanted to learn, but her parents did not have the money to allow her to stay in school. She remembered well the hard years of working in the laundry, when she was thirteen. To make up for her lack of schooling, she had spent every free moment since then reading. Now that she had children of her own, she insisted that her children be given the opportunity to avail themselves of a higher education and "become somebody," as she called it.

Ludwig passed the difficult entrance exam and was admitted to the *Gymnasium* in Pasing, one train stop from where we lived. Since Papa worked for the railroad, he was able to get a free rail pass for

Ludwig. Mama saved the tuition from the household money Papa gave her every payday.

Ludwig did well at the *Gymnasium*, and I loved, admired, and envied my big brother. I loved him when we did things together and he paid attention to me. I admired him when he played the piano and did things I couldn't do or when he wore his student cap to show that he was a *Gymnasiast*. Unfortunately, student caps were viewed as a sign of "elitism" and were soon prohibited by the Nazis in an effort to abolish class distinctions. I sometimes envied Ludwig when he was allowed to do things while I was told that I was too little, or whatever it was he did was for boys, not for girls.

One of the reasons for my admiration had to do with walking to the nearby milk store on Saturday mornings to buy milk and fresh hard rolls for breakfast. Sometimes Mama gave us change to also buy two soft pretzels. Back home, Mama sliced our pretzels, spread them with cold butter, and put them together sandwich-style for our special breakfast treat on that particular morning. They tasted absolutely wonderful.

Like the other customers, Ludwig and I brought our own aluminum milk can, which had a long carrying handle and a lid. Milk, fresh from the farm, was measured out in the desired quantity to be taken home and boiled. On the way home, Ludwig sometimes handed me the shopping net with the rolls, took the lid off the milk can, and swung it rapidly up over his head and around without spilling a drop. Not knowing anything about centrifugal force, I was always tremendously impressed and in awe of my older brother when he performed this "magic" for me.

Ludwig was big on experiments and when he allowed me to help him, he made me feel important, but sometimes we got into trouble.

Like many Germans, our parents enjoyed going for a walk on Sunday afternoons. After a busy work week, it was relaxing for them to look at the yards and flower gardens along the way. On this particular Sunday, my parents were going to stop by the Reisachs, leaving me in Ludwig's care. They told us we were allowed to cut some of the *Gesundheitskuchen,* bundt cake, Mama had baked for Sunday afternoon coffee. As soon as Mama and Papa had left, Ludwig announced: "I've built a cable car with the Erector Set I got for Christmas. It'll make eating the cake like an adventure. You get to help."

"What do I get to do?"

"Watch, this wire is going to be the cable. I'll anchor it here on the kitchen window. Now we'll string it all the way through the kitchen, out into the hall and fasten the other end on the pedestal of the staircase."

This accomplished, Ludwig proceeded to cut pieces of the cake. They didn't readily fit into the gondola, so Ludwig instructed me:

"You can roll these cake pieces into balls while I fix up the cable car."

Ludwig continued to set up the cable car and a little gondola while I dutifully rolled the cake pieces into balls and lined them up on two plates. Then I put a plate at each end of the cable.

"I'm done. Now what do I do?" I asked.

"You go out to the staircase in the hall. That'll be your cable car stop. I'll put a piece of cake in the gondola and send it to you. It's yours to eat. Then you put a piece of cake in the gondola, pull on the string and send it back for me to eat. OK? Here it comes."

The gondola loaded with the cake was swinging its way across the kitchen to the hallway. I giggled with delight when it arrived, and I unloaded my cake.

"This is neat. Now it's my turn to send you some cake," I mumbled, still munching cake.

"Yes, but be very careful. You have to balance it then pull steadily on the string; don't pull too hard or it'll spill," Ludwig instructed me.

I took his advice, slowly loaded the piece of cake into the gondola and barely pulled on the string. The gondola moved ever so slightly.

"You can pull harder," Ludwig urged, "or I'm never gonna get my cake."

"I'm afraid to . . . . It might spill."

But I pulled with a little more confidence and watched fascinated as the load slowly swayed over to Ludwig. Ludwig put another cake ball into the gondola. He was trying to show me that I really could pull a little faster when the gondola started tilting halfway across and the cake spilled onto the kitchen floor.

The afternoon went on with laughing and giggling, successes and failures. We had a great time.

"It's getting late. Mama and Papa will be home soon."

Ludwig started cleaning up. Too late. Mama and Papa had just unlocked the garden gate and were coming up the driveway. They were not happy when they saw the mess and, since Ludwig was older than I, he was the one Mama and Papa punished for being wasteful and irresponsible.

Another time when we were left alone, Ludwig decided to investigate electricity and was poking around in an outlet. I was standing behind Ludwig watching, when we both were thrown out into the hall. I had a bloody elbow and was scared to death.

After our parents returned, they discovered that there was no electricity anywhere in the house; all of the fuses had blown. Mama tried her best to calm Papa, who was not just angry but furious. From that time on, Ludwig and I were not allowed to stay at home alone. Sunday walks with our parents became obligatory.

Our activities didn't always get us into trouble.

Ludwig and I also were avid collectors of coupons from cigarette packages. Papa often brought us coupons from his colleagues who smoked. We sent the coupons in for books and packets of pictures. The books carried the storyline and provided spaces in which to glue the numbered pictures. It was always an exciting day when the books and pictures arrived, but Mama always made me wait until Ludwig came home from the *Gymnasium* before we could start to glue the beautiful color pictures into the books.

The stories in the books were interesting and dealt with various subjects. In this way we accumulated albums of the lifestyles and costumes of the Middle Ages, the flora and fauna of Germany, the men and women of history, the paintings of the Gothic, Baroque and early Renaissance periods. We treasured our "cigarette books," and I now realize that through these books, we acquired an early appreciation for art, history, and nature.

We both loved the outdoors, and summer would find us in the fields and meadow at the end of our block. Ludwig sometimes let me help him catch frogs, garter snakes, or crickets. At home he fixed up a terrarium for them. Catching flies and digging worms to feed them soon got to be a chore, and to Mama's relief Ludwig would return the "poor creatures," as Mama called them, back to nature.

We also had hedgehogs that we fed. They were easy to feed. We just put some milk and bread in a small dish and set it underneath our lilac bush. The hedgehogs usually were very punctual and came by about the same time every evening. All we had to do was to listen: They were some of the noisiest eaters, smacking and slurping like a full-grown pig.

Every season offered outdoor adventures for us. Winter was no exception.

In 1933, the day before school resumed after winter vacation, Ludwig was allowed to go ice skating with his friends. They went to the local gravel pit, where they always had lots of fun as they skated down a truck ramp at great speed. They spent the afternoon taking turns skating down and climbing back up. The time went fast and soon it would be time to go home, but before doing so, it was Ludwig's turn to skate down the incline. Unfortunately, this time his skate caught on something, and he fell. With his hands stretched out in front of him, he slid down, cutting the tendons of his middle, ring, and little finger of his left hand on a strip of razor-sharp metal protruding from the ice. Bleeding profusely and in acute pain, he wrapped his scarf around his hand. With his friends at his side, he ran home as fast as he could.

In the clinic, the wound was treated, and the tendons were reconnected. The following days were exhausting for the family. Mama held Ludwig, who was 12 years old at the time, through agonizing days and nights of pain. I could hear her singing and talking to him to try to comfort him.

A sister from the Catholic nuns came by the house daily to help check the bandages and look for any signs of infection. Without penicillin to ward off infection, it was questionable if his fingers, his hand, or even his arm could be saved.

In the end, Ludwig was able to keep his hand and also his fingers, even though they were stiff and useless. He was told that he would never be able to play the piano again, and it was very unlikely that he could fulfill his dream of becoming an engineer.

When this happened, I was not yet five years old. I remember feeling lost and somewhat abandoned as my dog, Lumpi, and I spent lots of time sitting on the front steps of our house while the grownups were taking care of Ludwig. In my own way, I worried about my brother, and I was glad to have Lumpi by my side. His coat felt soft and warm, and Lumpi was always a good listener.

After the worst pain had subsided and the healing process begun, Mama diligently worked with Ludwig to help him keep up with his studies. His friends and classmates, Anton B. and Alfred T., came and brought Ludwig his assignments and studied with him.

One day, they came into the living room, where Ludwig was studying, and Anton announced:

"Hey, Ludwig, did you hear? They've burnt books of undesirable authors."

"*Ja*, can you believe it?" Alfred exclaimed. "Sigmund Freud, Heinrich Heine, Franz Kafka, and lots of others, all their books went on the bonfire. The biggest bonfire was at the Berlin Opernplatz."

"*Ja. Im Westen Nichts Neues* by Erich Maria Remarque is also banned. My dad has a copy," Anton volunteered. "Maybe we should read it. I can bring it next time."

"*Ja*, bring it. We'll find out what's so bad about it," Ludwig agreed.

And that is how my brother and his friends came to read Remarque's anti-war novel "*All Quiet on the Western Front.*"

Even though Ludwig had worked tirelessly to try to keep up with his class, my parents wondered if it would be enough. The *Gymnasium* was extremely demanding, and Ludwig had missed three months of school.

Finally the day came when Ludwig was able to return to school and take the exams he had missed. Our family was ecstatic when we found out that he had passed all of his tests and was allowed to stay with his class.

However, that was not enough for Ludwig. He was determined to become an engineer and, for that, he needed hands that were able to work on the drawing board. He continuously massaged his stiff fingers, and manually bent them to try and grasp balls and various objects. He started to play simple exercises on the piano again and used his left hand to steady rulers when he was at the drawing board. Slowly, over the months and years, the fingers became more useful and eventually he was able to resume his piano lessons and pursue his dream of becoming an engineer.

My own schooling began the year after Ludwig's accident, in 1934. I was six years old when I entered first grade in the same public school that Ludwig had attended before he transferred to the *Gymnasium*. There was no kindergarten, no pre-orientation, but I was eager to start this new experience.

This is me on my first day of school in 1934.

To relieve any separation anxiety of the first day of school, Mama, as was customary for parents, gave me a large colorful, cone-shaped *Schultüte*, school bag, filled with candy, cookies, or fruit, as well as small school supplies such as pencils and erasers.

When Mama and I walked into my classroom, I felt like a tiny ant in a vast expanse. The classroom was large and so was our class. I was one among more than forty pupils.

In front of the classroom, a raised platform with two large blackboards on easels towered over me, one on each side. In the middle was the teacher's desk, and behind it, centered on the wall, hung a large wooden crucifix. The presence of the crucifix, and the fact that we began each school day with a short prayer, reminded us of how closely religious practice was woven into our lives.

This is my first-grade class, which had forty students.
Note the crucifix on the wall, which was later replaced
with a picture of *der Führer*.

My teacher was Fräulein Heinzelmeier, a rather young teacher compared to the rest of the teachers in our school. I remember how excited I was when Mama gave me my own wood-framed slate. From one string hung a little sponge to erase, and from the other, a small cloth for drying the slate. We wrote with a *Griffel*, a slim hard chalk stick with colorful glittery paper tightly wrapped around. To protect our *Griffel* from breaking, they were kept in a narrow wooden box with a sliding top. With these supplies, we learned to write in the old German script called *Sütterlin*.

On my back, I carried a *Schulranzen*, a leather case with straps to go over the shoulders, which held all of my school supplies, as well as a sandwich and a piece of fruit, to be eaten during recess in the school yard. There was no way to serve food at my school, so for the noon meal we all walked home to return at one o'clock for the afternoon lessons.

Along with the basics, Fräulein Heinzelmeier also taught us a very simple kind of embroidery done on wide-meshed stiff material. I liked needlework and was very proud when Mama displayed the doily in the living room in spite of the ghastly color combination I had picked out.

Every day before I left the house to walk to school, Mama would give me explicit instructions on how to cross the street, how to behave in school, and admonish me not to talk to strangers. Last, she always asked:

"Do you have a clean handkerchief? Is your underwear clean?"

I think I could have gotten by with a few spots on my dress, but God forbid that the underwear wouldn't be clean or that there was no clean handkerchief in my pocket.

My first year in school was happy. I loved the soft-spoken Fräulein Heinzelmeier and often brought her flowers from Mama's garden. When I found out that I would have Fräulein Heinzelmeier again in second grade, I was overjoyed.

I don't remember our school ever being closed because of snow. We walked to school no matter how much snow we had. Often, by the time we got to school, our shoes and stockings were wet and our feet felt like icicles. The teacher would have us line up our shoes along the radiators so that they might dry before we had to start our walk home.

I recall one winter morning after an unusually heavy snowfall. Our suburb's lone horse-drawn snowplow had only been able to clear a narrow lane in the middle of the street. My friend Erna and I were trudging through the snow on our way to school. Suddenly, we heard sleigh bells approaching from behind.

"Whoa." The horse-drawn sleigh came to a stop.

"There's room for you two, if you're not too heavy for the horse," Herr Knobling chuckled as he invited us. He was taking his daughter Luise, who was in my grade, to school.

Erna and I, both skinny like bean poles, giggled as we got on and squeezed in next to Luise.

We felt special as we rode through the snow-covered streets, our legs and feet warm and snug under the huge lap robe.

"Thanks for the ride, Herr Knobling," we said, jumping off the sleigh at the school.

"I'll be back after school to pick all of you up," he offered. That was one snowy winter day we didn't have to dry our shoes by the radiator.

These are some of my memories of Ludwig's and my early school years. Ludwig's accident made me aware early on how much I loved my brother, and it strengthened our bond. The memories of these happy and sheltered years sustained both Ludwig and me during the dark war years to come.

While I was able to continue my schooling during the war, Ludwig's ambition to become an engineer was tested to the limit. Memories of happier days enabled him to survive unimaginable hardships before he could finalize his dream.

Chapter 10

The Problem with Sacrifices

It was April 1937 and, judging by the flurry of activity, there was going to be a special day or a special occasion in the Heider household near Munich, Germany.

For several days, not only had a *Störnäherin*, a woman who sews at her customer's house, been hired, but also a cleaning lady. The carpet runners from the various rooms had been carried outside, hung over the children's gym bar in the yard and thoroughly beaten with the oval rattan carpet beater.

The house smelled of freshly waxed floors that had been buffed with the "*Blocker*" until one was almost blinded by their shine. Papa had made sure that any debris from the early spring storms had been cleared away in the yard.

Recipes had been selected and the necessary shopping done. Mama had baked cake layers for various *Torten,* many-layered cakes with rich butter cream fillings, in the large wood-burning stove, without any temperature control or thermometer of any kind. Somehow, Mama always seemed to know when the oven temperature was right.

Even my brother, Ludwig, was enlisted to fill and decorate the various *Torten.* The event that occasioned all this activity was my First Holy Communion in the Catholic Church. I was nine years old.

In religion class in school, we had been studying the Catechism to prepare for this day. We also were prepared to go to confession, and this was what was troubling me. I was very concerned about what things I had to confess.

There was the time during summer vacation when I had spent a couple of weeks with my cousins Bettie and Liesel near Regensburg. The three of us were just three months apart in age and skinny as rails. Some of our classmates actually had curves, while we had no signs of budding breasts. We felt this to be a terrible lack. In our class, there were rumors of all the things that were going to happen to us, more specifically to our bodies, but we had no clue as to when or how. No one had enlightened us about the monthlies or hormones.

Liesel had heard rumors that in order to make the breasts grow, one needed to wash and rub the chest every morning with icy cold water. Commiserating, the three of us went through this cold water ritual every morning in the bathroom, shivering and teeth chattering.

When it was time for me to go back home, we promised each other to continue this Spartan treatment until we would see each other again next vacation. We were certain that we would then be blessed with shapely breasts.

Now, with the prospect of having to make my confession, I was worried.

Those were impure thoughts, weren't they? Just how much of this would I have to tell the priest? Could I go to another church and confess? . . . Somewhere where the priest didn't know me? . . . Gosh, the Protestants sure have it easy. They don't have to go to confession . . . .

On the day of confession, as I entered the church, the wooden confessional booth I had passed so callously before now loomed menacingly in front of me.

In spite of my worries, I survived confession. The priest behind the wooden grill didn't seem the least bit interested in the details of my impure thoughts. He actually sounded almost bored as he gave me my penance and absolution. Immensely relieved, I left the confessional.

When the day of my First Holy Communion finally came, I was excited and full of eager anticipation. It was a lovely April morning, but quite cool, so I wore a white pleated cape over the white dress our seamstress had sewed for me. A purse, made from the same material as the cape, and white gloves completed the outfit. My head was encircled by a wreath of white silk flowers, and on each of my almost waist-length braids was a big white bow.

In one hand, I carried a tall white candle with silver decorations and in the other, a rosary and a white leather prayer book from my parents. I also wore a necklace with a silver cross, a very special gift from Mama.

This is me, on the day of my First Communion.
My brother, Ludwig, took this picture.

Julie, my eighteen-year old cousin, was my godmother. She arrived with her mother, Aunt Martha. Julie was always the perfect young lady. She spoke in a soft modulated voice, never laughed out loud, and was always perfectly groomed.

I had ambivalent feelings about Julie. While I loved Julie dearly, I sometimes resented this high level of "perfection," especially when I was told by Mama to be less boisterous and to try to be more like Julie.

"I debated whether to give you this present now so that you can wear it to church, or keep it until later," Julie explained as she put a pretty gold watch on my wrist. "I don't want it to distract you from saying your prayers during Mass."

"Oh, Julie, it's so beautiful, thank you very much. I will say my prayers . . . and even some extra ones," I hastened to promise.

Aunt Therese and Uncle Georg, as well as other relatives, had also arrived. I shook hands with every new arrival. I was a big girl now and no longer obligated to curtsy to visitors as I did when I was little. Congratulatory cards and several presents were stacked on the desk in the living room. After excited greetings all around, everyone walked to the church where the First Communion Mass was to be celebrated.

While the communicants met in the sacristy, their families took seats in the church, which was beautifully decorated with white flowers, bouffant white ribbons, and lots of greenery. People were crowding into the church till finally there was only standing room in the back.

We, the communicants, filed into the church to the strains of organ preludes and then took our places in the front pews reserved for us. The scent of incense, the chanting of the priests, and the singing of the worshippers filled the church. Our faces had a solemn glow as we received the Host for the first time. I was swept up in the ceremony and vowed to myself to study hard at school, not to procrastinate with homework, and to try to be more helpful to Mama, maybe even try to emulate Julie, and, most of all, to think only pure thoughts in order to remain in my state of grace.

After Mass, everyone gathered at our house for a festive meal. Mama served another one of my favorite soups, pancake soup with freshly chopped parsley on top. This was followed by a beef loin roast with sour cream gravy and *Spätzle*. The salads were butter lettuce with an herb dressing, a cucumber salad, and a red beet salad. It was a truly festive meal. Everyone raised a glass of wine as Julie made a befitting toast to me, her godchild.

After dinner, I was allowed to open the rest of my presents, and photos were taken to commemorate this important milestone. The afternoon passed quickly and after a stroll in the yard, where the men had a cigar or cigarette and looked at the new plantings, it was time for the customary Sunday afternoon coffee.

Mama had set a festive table with a crisp white damask tablecloth, fresh flowers, and my christening china. The various delectable *Torten* were served, and bowls of whipped cream were passed around to lavish on the fruit tarts, and also to crown each cup of coffee. All this was followed by Mama's homemade black currant liqueur. The conversation flowed, and I felt very special. I loved having all of the family together and basked in the attention showered upon me.

One of the communion presents I had received was a richly illustrated book about the lives of some women saints. I was delighted with the gift because saints played an important part in my life as they did in the lives of many others in the predominantly Catholic region of Bavaria.

In fact, to be baptized in the Catholic Church, one had to be named after a saint. I was named after Saint Anna and Saint Elisabeth—Anneliese being a combination of those two names.

In Bavaria, we celebrated our name day, the day assigned to a saint. For me, the name day was Saint Anna's Day, July 26, when I would receive cards or presents of flowers, sweets or other small gifts, just as others did on their name days.

During the next few weeks, I read in the saint book about Saint Anna, the mother of the Virgin Mary, Saint Barbara, Saint Klara of Assisi, and many others. I was deeply impressed as I read about Saint Elisabeth, the daughter of King Andrew II of Hungary. Betrothed to Louis IV of Thuringia, Elisabeth was sent to live at her future husband's court at the tender age of four. When Elisabeth was fourteen, she and Louis were married. By the time she was twenty she was widowed with two children. Elisabeth ministered to the poor, the sick, and the very young, giving away her wealth to better their lives. She died in poverty at the age of twenty-four.

I was so inspired by the accounts in this book that I decided I should become a nun and help relieve misery and suffering. I had no clue how to go about becoming a nun, and I was even more naïve about a life of sacrifice.

To prepare myself for this noble life, I resolved to pray several times a day as nuns do, to be very obedient, to do extra work around the house, to not tease Ludwig, and to be nice to all of the kids in school, especially the ones I had previously ignored.

I also needed to make actual sacrifices. What sacrifices could I make? Working in the garden probably would not count because I liked to work with the flowers, and anything I liked probably could not be counted as a sacrifice.

Meanwhile, Mama wondered what could be wrong with me. She said I had not been myself lately. Instead of coming home from school, tearing off my school clothes, jumping into my outdoor clothes, and running out to play with the kids in the neighborhood, I spent much more time in the house. I was actually volunteering to do extra jobs instead of the usual procrastinations.

"Did something happen at school, or did you have a fight with your friend Johanna?" Mama wanted to know. "You're not sick, I hope," and, feeling my forehead, she said, "No, you don't seem to have a fever."

"I'm OK. I just have lots to do." Saying all those prayers and volunteering was really keeping me busy.

"Know what? There's a Shirley Temple movie coming to the Ufa Palast Theater. I think we should go see it next Saturday," Mama coaxed.

My eyes lit up but only for a moment. Remembering my new resolve, with a rather uncertain voice I answered, "I don't think I can go."

I know Mama was really puzzled now. I never, ever turned down a Shirley Temple movie. In fact, most of the time, I would wheedle Mama into going a second and often a third time. We had seen every Shirley Temple movie together at least twice.

I really wanted to see the movie. *But I am supposed to make sacrifices . . . . Not going to the Shirley Temple movie would certainly have to count as a big sacrifice . . . . Gee, I didn't know this making sacrifices business was this hard.*

The thought of not seeing a movie with Shirley Temple haunted me all weekend. On Monday in school, one of my classmates was bragging about going with her older sister. That did it. *Maybe I could go and see the movie only once and sacrifice going to see it the second time,* I rationalized.

After school I asked Mama if we could still go to see the movie on Saturday. And so we did.

Mama actually had no reason to worry. My religious fervor did not last very long.

After a few weeks of saying prayers several times a day, offering to do extra jobs around the house, preparing myself for this life of denial and hardships got to be a real chore. *There are just so many things to give up, . . . but Mama always tells me to finish what I start . . . but I really didn't start it, I just tried it. I wonder: will God punish me? I really don't think I'd make a very good nun . . . and I'm sure God doesn't want a bad nun.*

So, after considerable debate, I finally decided that planning my future could perhaps wait a while and went back to being myself. However, going to Mass on Sunday and saying the required prayers at night and at mealtime didn't prevent me from getting into a little trouble now and then.

Pfannkuchensuppe—Pancake Soup

We often asked Mama to make this soup for us.

Cooled thin pancakes* (see basic pancake recipe below)
Chicken broth
Chopped parsley or chives for garnish

Roll up cooled pancakes and cut into thin strips, like noodles. Store in refrigerator.

When ready to serve, put the pancake strips into individual soup bowls, pour hot chicken broth over the pancake strips, and sprinkle with chopped parsley or chives. Serve immediately.

Pfannkuchen—Basic Pancakes

To ensure tender pancakes, this batter should be prepared and refrigerated an hour or two before frying the pancakes. Makes about 10 pancakes.

1 cup all-purpose flour
Dash of salt
2 eggs
1½ cup milk
Oil for frying

Mix together all ingredients well. Batter should be consistency of thick cream. Heat a small amount of oil in frying pan. Pour in a small amount of batter, tilting to cover all of pan. Brown lightly on each side and remove.

Oma Heider's *Spätzle*

3 cups flour
1/2 teaspoon salt
4 eggs
1¼ cup milk*
3 tablespoons freshly grated Parmesan cheese
Butter
Additional Parmesan cheese (optional)
Chopped chives (optional)

Mix together flour, salt, eggs, milk, and Parmesan cheese in large mixer bowl and beat until very smooth. Bring 3 quarts of water to a full boil. Add one-half teaspoon salt.

Press dough in batches through a *Spätzle* press or a colander with large holes, directly into the boiling water. Stir gently to keep *Spätzle* from sticking to each other. Boil briskly for 2 to 3 minutes. *Spätzle* are done when they float. Boiling them too long will make them sticky. Drain and rinse. (They can be made a day ahead up to this point.) Sprinkle with chives and extra cheese and serve immediately.

If made ahead, melt butter in non-stick skillet, add Spätzle and heat through. Add extra cheese and chives and serve.

* Depending on the size of the holes in your colander, you may need to add more milk to batter.

Gurkensalat—Cucumber Salad

2 cucumbers, peeled and sliced thin
Salt to taste
2½ tablespoons vinegar
Pepper to taste
Pinch of sugar
1 tablespoon chopped onion (optional)
1/2 teaspoon fresh chopped dill weed, or 1/4 teaspoon dried
Fresh chopped chives

Place the sliced cucumbers in a bowl and sprinkle with salt. Let stand for 15 minutes. Drain off some of the liquid if necessary. Add the rest of the ingredients and serve.

This can be added to the Bavarian potato salad.

Rote Rübensalat—Beet Salad

3 to 4 red beets
Water
2 tablespoons vinegar
1 teaspoon salt

Dressing:
1/4 cup water
1/4 cup vinegar
2 tablespoons sugar
1 teaspoon caraway seed
2 tablespoons chopped onion

Put beets in pan with enough water to cover. Add vinegar and salt. Boil until beets are tender. Peel the beets while still warm. Slice beets and pour the dressing over.

This salad is best if allowed to marinate 8 hours or overnight.

Chapter 11

The Cousin from America

During my early years, most of my mother's relatives lived in the United States. Mama's younger sister Katherine had immigrated to the United States after World War I in search of work.

Later on, in 1929, Mama's youngest sister Marie, her husband, Willie, and their four-year-old daughter, my cousin Mariele, followed Katherine to the United States. Marie and Willie made their home in a suburb of Westchester, New York.

Willie worked as an auto mechanic, and Marie cleaned homes for several wealthy families in Scarsdale. Mariele, a well-mannered and obedient child, went along to the various jobs and colored or played while Marie worked. Marie's employers enjoyed having the pretty little girl around and did not object to Marie bringing her to work.

Marie and Willie Riefler worked hard. After they paid the day-to-day expenses, they also were able to put some money aside each month. At home, they continued to speak their native German with their daughter, but they also learned the English language in order to function in their adopted country.

Marie was glad to be near her sister Katherine, but she missed her older sister, my mother. Life in the big city of New York was hectic compared to the slower-paced life in the Lake Constance region of Germany, where Marie used to get up in the morning to watch the sun come up over the snowcapped peaks of the Alps.

In 1933, the family returned to Germany for a visit, and they bought a lot on Theresienstrasse, in the suburb of Munich where we lived. It was just four houses down the street from our house. Three years later, they sent Papa the plans for their new house. Papa hired a contractor and oversaw the construction. When the house was finished, it was leased for a year to the Moser family while Willie and Marie settled their affairs in New York.

In 1937, Willie was hired as a mechanic by the railroad in Munich. He had worked for the railroad before he and his family immigrated to the United States. The railroad not only gave him a job, but he also received credit for his previous years of work with them. Because his wife, Marie, and his daughter, Mariele, were still in New York, Uncle Willie stayed with us.

Finally, in the early spring of 1938, Uncle Willie announced that his wife and daughter, along with all of their steamer trunks, were on a ship bound for Bremerhaven. The Mosers still lived in my aunt and uncle's house, even though their lease had expired a month ago. Herr Moser was a loyal party member in the SA, and he refused to move out for "the Americans."

So not only Uncle Willie, but also Aunt Marie and my cousin Mariele were going to stay with us. That was exciting news for me. It would be like having an older sister.

The day before their arrival, Papa and Uncle Willie put a bed and a dresser for Mariele in my room. I pleaded to be allowed to delay my bedtime in order to meet them, but I was told that Aunt Marie and Mariele would arrive very late from Bremerhaven. Tomorrow was a school day. I had to go to bed.

The next day at breakfast I expected to see my cousin, but Mariele had been exhausted from the trip and was still sleeping. I did meet my Aunt Marie, who took me into the living room, where Mariele was sleeping on the couch, so that I could at least have a glimpse of my cousin, whom I had not seen since I was five years old.

In school, it was difficult for me to pay attention; I couldn't wait for the school day to be over. Of course, I had told all of my friends about the arrival of my cousin from America. When school was finally over, I ran home as fast as my legs would carry me.

"Where is my cousin? I want a see her," the words literally exploded as I came in the door.

"Slow down. Mariele is upstairs in your room putting some of her things away," Mama tried to explain, but I was already half-way up the stairs.

"Hi, and thanks for sharing your room," Mariele greeted me.

"I've been waiting for you ever since your Papa came last year," I confessed and went on: "Mama said we'll have Easter dinner together. Won't that be neat?"

"Yes . . . . I'm almost unpacked. Your mom told me you like Shirley Temple. I brought several scrapbooks of movie stars from the States . . . . Wanta see them?"

"Wow! Yes, of course."

Soon we were absorbed in Mariele's scrapbooks. There was not only Shirley Temple, but also Deanna Durbin, Jane Withers, and glamorous stars like Carole Lombard, Don Ameche, and Jean Harlow. Whole pages of their glamorous lifestyles, their luxurious homes, their beautiful cars, and shots on movie locations unfolded before me.

Mariele also had a scrapbook with comic strips. The German papers did not carry comics, and I was enthralled. Mariele translated the speech balloons for me. Later, I could go back and recreate the stories on my own. That is how I became acquainted with the Little King, Blondie, and Popeye. All this was a wonderful new world for me. I savored these hours with Mariele.

In the course of the next few weeks, we also looked at picture albums of Mariele's life in America. In one picture, Mariele and her friend Jane were standing in front of Mariele's family's car. I didn't know anyone in our middle-class neighborhood who had a car. That is when I decided that America must be wonderful. Everyone seemed to have a car, was beautiful, and must be rich.

Mariele and her parents had arrived a few weeks before Easter, and we had been looking forward to celebrating Easter together. It was the day before Easter, and Mama said it was time to dye the Easter eggs. Mariele and I were allowed to help.

To dye the eggs, Mama used the paper-like skins of yellow onions and added them to the boiling water for yellow eggs. In another pot, Mama had boiled beets for beet salad and the water was used to dye red eggs. Spinach gave us green eggs.

When we came home after church on Easter Sunday, I found a big chocolate Easter bunny and also an Easter lamb, along with the traditional colored eggs, in my basket. The chocolate bunny did not last too long; I shared it with Ludwig and Mariele. The Easter lamb, however, was so beautiful that I put it on top of the tall dresser in my bedroom, so I could admire it.

For our Easter dinner, Mama and Aunt Marie had prepared pork Schnitzel, potato salad mixed with early lamb's lettuce, and a cabbage salad. She also had opened a jar of the quince compote that she had put up last fall. In the afternoon, while the adults played cards and exchanged stories about their life during the time they had been apart, Ludwig, Mariele and I played games. At the 4 o'clock coffee hour, Mama served an Easter *Torte*, rich with butter cream frosting, while Aunt Marie poured the coffee and passed the whipped cream. Easter day had been such a satisfying experience in the midst of both families, I hated for it to end.

Since Easter Monday is also a legal holiday in Bavaria, we did not have school the next day.

Mariele and I decided to look at her scrapbooks and then also read some comics. I was intrigued with Mariele's accent.

"You talk different, . . . but I like it," I told Mariele.

"I guess I do have an accent. I really need help with my German. I can speak OK, but I don't know how to write German and after Easter vacation I'll start school. Will you help me?" she asked.

"Sure. Maybe you can teach me some English words," I offered.

In New York, Mariele had to take violin lessons, which she despised. Now her parents allowed Mariele to stop taking violin lessons in order to improve her German as quickly as possible. Both Mariele and I thought that was an excellent trade-off, and soon we were busy reading and writing German.

One day, Mariele came home from school all excited. She had met a girl named Ingrid, who was a year older than she. I knew Ingrid. She lived around the corner in the next street. Since she was four years older than I was, she had never paid much attention to me nor I to her. Ingrid was friendly, and I always thought she was nice . . . until now. I was jealous and resented anyone taking up Mariele's time. I wanted to keep my cousin all to myself. It took a little lecture from Mama and some time for me to get used to having Ingrid around.

Since Mariele's arrival, our house was a lot more fun. One of the reasons for this was the pranks Mariele and I played on my brother. Of course, Ludwig was always quick to retaliate. Ludwig's bedroom was across the hall from the one Mariele and I shared. One time, Ludwig put sneezing powder under our pillows. Mariele and I sneezed until tears ran down our cheeks.

Another time Ludwig attached strings to the bottom corner of our feather beds, hiding the strings under the carpet runner that led through the hall into his room. Just when Mariele and I had settled down to go to sleep, he pulled on the strings, and off came our covers.

Sometimes it was Ludwig's craving for sweets that got him into trouble. Several weeks after Easter, I noticed that my Easter lamb was leaning backward. I tried to rectify the situation, but the lamb fell over. The whole back side was missing; the front shell had been propped up with little sticks. It didn't take long to figure out that the culprit was Ludwig, whose sweet tooth had gotten the better of him.

While we, the young people, enjoyed the two families living under one roof, Mariele's parents were eager to take possession of their own house. It had been six months, and the Mosers still had not moved out. After much waiting and putting up with red tape, Uncle Willie proved that his family still had German citizenship, and he finally received permission to move his family into their home.

I was not happy about losing my roommate. Mariele and I had become very close. My consolation was that their house was only four houses down the street from us, and Aunt Marie promised me that I could spend some weekends with Mariele.

When I helped Mariele unpack and settle into her room in the new house, I was intrigued with the things she had brought from America. One was a bedspread made out of little pieces of material. I had never seen anything like it in Germany. It had a star pattern, and Mariele called it a quilt. In front of her bed was a heavy horsehair rug. Her clothes also were quite different. I was fascinated by it all.

Besides learning about things typically American, I also became acquainted with some new dishes. On one of my sleepovers, Aunt Marie made Italian spaghetti and meatballs. She said it was a recipe from Aunt Katherine, whose husband was of Italian heritage. I loved the meal and begged Mama to try and make it.

Mama, who was an excellent cook, surprised us one day and served it to our family. We all liked the meal, so Mama decided to plant basil in her herb garden, for use in her new Italian recipe.

Mariele did miss some of the things they had in the United States, like corn-on-the cob, Jell-O, popcorn, and her favorite drink, ginger ale.

While we were cousins, Mariele and I looked enough alike that people sometimes thought we were sisters. They referred to us as day and night, since she was blonde and I was dark. She was quiet while I was rambunctious, as Mama called it.

Many years later, Mariele reminded me of how Mama used to fix Boston Bibb lettuce with vinaigrette dressing liberally sprinkled with chopped chives and fresh herbs from the garden. I loved this tangy dressing and often drank the leftover dressing. Mariele confessed that she started drinking it, too, because she thought it would make her spunkier, like me. We both had a good laugh at that, especially when I told her that I tried in vain to be more quiet and patient, like she was, in order to improve my "approval rating" with Mama.

My cousin Mariele became very special to me. Living with us for a few months and then moving to a house close to us, Mariele early on aroused my interest in America and the American lifestyle. This interest also made me eager to learn the English language, a skill that would open doors for me after the war and eventually lead me across the ocean to a new life.

Here we are on Christmas 1937 when Uncle Willie was
living with us. From left: Herr Soller, Uncle Willie,
Papa, me, Mama, and Ludwig.

Schweineschnitzel—Pork Schnitzel

4 pork loin slices, 1/2-inch thick
Salt and pepper
Flour
1 egg mixed with 2 tablespoons water, lightly beaten
Bread crumbs
Vegetable oil
Lemon slices
Parsley for garnish

Pound cutlets until thin. Sprinkle with salt and pepper. Dredge each cutlet with flour, then dip in egg wash and dredge in bread crumbs. Let the breaded cutlets rest for 30 minutes on a sheet of wax paper.

Heat oil in skillet and fry cutlets until done, turning once. This takes about 15 minutes. Garnish with lemon slices and parsley sprigs. When served, squeeze the lemon juice over the Schnitzel.

Schnitzel are good served with salads and parsley potatoes.

Chapter 12

Kristallnacht:
Broken Glass and Shattered Lives

The easy days of summer vacation were almost over. My brother, Ludwig, and I needed school supplies and some new clothes.

Mama and I were on the train to Munich because Mama wanted to take advantage of the sales happening in all the big department stores. We didn't often go to the city, and I always looked forward to the train ride. I listened to the steady staccato rhythm of the train as the landscape rushed by and watched the people as they got on and off the train.

Today, a lady and her German shepherd dog got on at the next stop. I was immediately fascinated. I knew I shouldn't stare, but my eyes kept going back to the beautiful animal. The dog immediately responded to the woman's command to lie down on the floor of the train. I wanted to ask her if I could pet him, but I knew that would be too forward. Mama would not allow it. Mama had been bitten by a dog once and while she tolerated our dog, Lumpi, and always treated him kindly, she was not fond of dogs. Papa, on the other hand, liked all dogs. I would have to tell him about this beautiful, well-trained dog when we got home tonight.

When we arrived in Munich, the noises of a busy city immediately surrounded us. People were hurrying in every direction, cars were honking at jaywalkers, and street fruit and vegetable sellers were hawking the products on their carts. There was so much to see, and I tried to take it all in.

What I looked forward to most of all was to have lunch in the restaurant of the Tietz Department store. Unless we were on a trip during summer vacation, we never went out to eat, so for me, lunch at Tietz's was a rare occurrence. As we were walking down Kaufinger Street, I was already contemplating what wonderful treats I might possibly order.

After we had been to several other stores, we arrived at the Tietz Department store to finish our shopping and to have lunch. With all the pedestrians on the sidewalk, we had not noticed the two men wearing the brown-shirt uniform of the SA, the Nazi Party's militia, until they were in front of us. They had stationed themselves on both sides of the store entrance and, as we approached the big revolving door, they stepped in front of us:

"Germans don't shop in Jewish stores," they hissed, denying us entrance to the store.

No one was allowed to enter.

Mama said nothing, just reached for my hand and quickly turned around. Obediently, she hurried away with me.

"Why can't we go in?" I asked, bewildered.

"Hush, don't ask, just keep on walking. We'll go to Oberpollinger" was all she said.

I could tell Mama was upset, and deep down I felt something was terribly wrong.

Even though Mama was always friendly and pleasant, she was not afraid to stand up for herself. I was confused. Why had she walked away, meek as a lamb?

Silently, we made our way back to Oberpollinger's. We entered the store that was packed with customers who, like us, had been turned away from Tietz's. It was a challenge to make our way to the escalator amid the throng of people. The restaurant, too, was crowded. After some time, we finally managed to get a table. It was a relief to sit down, but disturbing thoughts crowded my mind. I could not forget the two SA men and the fact that everyone obeyed their command without so much as a word.

"I know you had looked forward to eating at Tietz's," Mama broke the silence. "You saw what happened. The owners are Jewish. I always liked to shop there, but they won't let us shop there anymore." There was a tone of resignation in her voice.

"Why can they stop us? Why can't we shop in Jewish stores?"

"There's nothing we can do about it. People who don't obey orders are punished severely."

Was Mama too upset, or too afraid, to talk to me about it? I looked at the long glass counter filled with delectable desserts to distract from the uncomfortable, heavy silence.

I had so many questions: *Who were "they?" The Brown Shirts? The National Socialist Party? Why? Why did "they" care where we shopped? Why were the Jews different from the French, the Italians, or other nationalities? In religion class, the priest told us that God loves everyone. Doesn't that include the Jews? Jesus was a Jew, so God must love Jews, too.*

My head was full of questions, but I didn't know who I could ask. Instinctively, I knew that Mama didn't want to say any more. I'd better not ask my teacher. He often wore his brown shirt uniform to school.

My thoughts were interrupted by the waitress ready to take our order. Mama ordered my favorite lunch, but when the waitress brought it, it didn't taste the same. There was a knot in my stomach that prevented me from savoring my food. This was not the happy lunch of other times, when we talked and laughed. Instead, I sensed Mama's fear, her anger and confusion, as well as her feeling of impotence at having to walk away silently. My instincts told me that those happy times were in the past and would never come back. It was like a menacing cloud had suddenly obscured my happy sky.

I was glad when the waitress brought our bill, Mama paid, and we left the restaurant. Neither Mama nor I found much joy in the rest of our shopping. Mama finished her shopping list without the usual enthusiasm, and I wanted nothing more than to be home. Wearily, we trudged to the train station to catch the next train home.

"How was the shopping?" Papa inquired when we got home.

"Let me get some of these things unpacked, then we'll talk," was Mama's wary reply.

I was no longer excited to tell Papa about the dog on the train. Instead, I ran upstairs to my room and cried bitter tears of anger, helplessness, and futility. I fervently wished my brother was home, but he was on a bicycle trip through Germany with his friends Anton and Alfred.

That evening, after the supper dishes had been cleared, I went into the living room to immerse myself in Ludwig's latest Karl May book—to experience the freedom of the American frontier, to scout with the Indian tribes along the Mississippi, and to hear the thundering herds of wild buffalo stampede across the endless prairie.

I could not help, however, to be aware of my parent's guarded voices and to hear my mother say, "One day there will be a horrible accounting for this."

I could only surmise that she was talking about what had happened at the department store. I put my book aside. I could not concentrate my thoughts on reading. All of my unanswered questions were there to haunt me. My world was changing, and I was not sure how or why.

Sometime after our shopping trip, on November 9, 1938, the infamous *Kristallnacht*, the "Night of Broken Glass," was unleashed against Germany's Jews. On that night, Jewish homes were broken into, Jewish people were arrested, synagogues were burned, and the glass of broken Jewish store windows carpeted the streets of Munich and other cities.

Whenever we shopped in Munich after that, we walked past the boarded-up windows of the Tietz department store, angry at the outrage that happened on that night, unable to do anything about it.

Were the owners arrested and sent to a concentration camp? Or were they among the ones who were given the option to flee to another country by giving up all of their wealth to the Nazi regime? We never found out.

Chapter 13

Schooldays and Darkening Shadows

School remained the central activity of my young life, which was colored by the events of the school day and the rhythms of the school year.

Not all my school days were happy ones. Both the changing political scene, as well as some other events, created unhappiness in my relatively idyllic young life. I came to learn as well that even those times that seem happy may be deceptively so when the larger context is known.

One fall, I don't remember what grade I was in, when I came back to school, the crucifix in our classroom had been replaced with a picture of the *Führer*. The school day now started with a "*Heil Hitler*" with our right arm raised in a salute, instead of the usual morning prayer.

I do remember one particular year of my elementary schooling and the eventful summer that followed. In our sewing and needlework class, we were learning to knit white knee-highs in the cable pattern. This pattern presented quite a challenge for us ten year olds. It required constant concentration and counting.

By the time most of us had finished our socks, they were no longer white but gray from the many times we had knit and re-knit them. Mine, too, were different shades of white and gray, and one stocking was a good inch longer than the other, so I had to unravel and re-knit it until both were finally of equal length. Most of us finally mastered the cable pattern, but more important for me, I had developed a love for knitting which lasted all of my life.

In the past, I had always received a "1," or an A in the American grading system, in needlework. My mother was therefore very surprised when I came home with a failing grade. After all, my socks had turned out very nice—after they had been washed. Like other parents in the early 1930s, my parents did not question a teacher as to why a certain grade was given. There were no parent-teacher conferences, and there was no PTA. The reason for my failing grade, therefore, remained a mystery to my parents until many years later, when I finally told them that the reason for my failure was the following incident:

In grade school, we had two recesses during the school day, the big and the little break. During the big break, we were outside and ate our snacks, which we brought from home in a brown paper bag. On this particular day, we were out in the schoolyard for our snack break as usual. Our next class was sewing and needlework. My friend Johanna and I had just finished our snack, when Johanna pointed to the church next to our school,

"Hey, Anneliese, look at the coach with the white horses."

Looking up, I saw a bride getting out of the carriage and being escorted into the church.

"I've never been to a wedding, have you?" I asked her.

"No."

Almost on command, we both ran out of the schoolyard and over to the church.

Standing in the back, we watched in awe as the wedding ceremony began. We just knew the bride was beautiful, even though we really couldn't see her under the veil. Her gown's long train was carried by a little boy dressed in a black suit. The groom was very handsome, and we couldn't take our eyes off the couple.

It was so romantic, we were mesmerized. Of course, we had not heard the bell signaling the end of recess. By the time we finally left the church and got back to school, the sewing and needlework class was over.

The next day, the teacher decided to let everyone know that skipping her class had dire consequences. We each were to receive two *Tatzen,* hits on the palm of each hand, with a long bamboo stick.

I was first. She told me to hold out my hand, palm up. As if I didn't know. I had seen other kids punished in this way, but this was the first time for Johanna and me.

The first time she hit each hand it stung so much that tears came into my eyes, even though I had gritted my teeth to prepare myself. I didn't want the other kids to see me cry, but by the time the teacher had administered three, I couldn't handle any more and before the fourth hit I flinched and pulled my hand back. It was an automatic reaction to avoid more pain. I didn't mean for the teacher to hit her knee with the stick. The teacher thought I had done it on purpose. She was really furious. Holding on to my hand she administered the legal limit, six *Tatzen*, instead of four.

Tears running down my face and totally humiliated, I slunk back to my seat, put my head in my arms on the desk and broke down and cried. I wanted to die.

The sound of Johanna receiving her four *Tatzen* went through me, and I winced each time. After school, Johanna and I used back roads to get home. We didn't want to see anyone from school who knew about our shame.

At home, I locked myself in the bathroom and soaked my burning hands in cold water to reduce the swelling and at supper time it was difficult to manipulate the silverware with my painful, swollen hands. I hoped my parents wouldn't notice because I knew I would receive no support from my parents in complaints about my teachers. They would tell me to obey and not get into trouble if I didn't want to get punished.

In my humiliation and frustration I was thinking: *It's always obey and respect your elders . . . give your seat up for a grownup on the train or streetcar . . . don't stare . . . clean your plate . . . if a grownup drops something, pick it up . . . don't talk back . . . open doors for grownups . . . close the doors quietly . . . wait your turn . . . be helpful . . . "speak up" if you didn't say anything . . . or "children should be seen, not heard" if you said too much. Does anyone ever tell me to go and have some fun?*

As I often did when I was troubled, I took solace that night in one of Ludwig's Karl May books. My favorites were the books of Winnetou, the noble savage, and his white blood brother Old Shatterhand. Even though he had never visited the American "Wild West" before writing his books, Karl May described its rivers and geography very realistically. I lost myself in the book, and my swollen hands didn't sting quite as much anymore.

Every day as Johanna and I walked to school, we relived that punishment. I was glad when school was out, and summer activities vied for my attention. Just before vacation began, my maternal grandmother came to say good-bye to us. She was sailing to America on one of the transatlantic ocean liners to visit her daughter, my Aunt Katherine. I was excited and longed to go to America with her.

While that was not possible, a summer program from our church helped to put the school punishment and the longing to visit my relatives in America behind me.

Church attendance was an important part of our Sunday activities. Mama usually went to early Mass, so she would get back in time to prepare the noon meal. Papa, Ludwig, and I went to the late service at eleven o'clock.

Being the dedicated church members that they were, it was not surprising that, when our church appealed to its parishioners to invite a handicapped child from a poor family to spend one Sunday a month with them, my parents had volunteered. That is how we met Franz, a rather lanky twelve year old who dragged one of his feet when he walked and whose arm and hand movements were rather erratic. Franz was from a family of eight, he had two sisters and three brothers.

That summer, one Sunday of each month his older brother brought him to church and after Mass, Franz came home with us for Sunday dinner, which he obviously relished. Following the meal, we played simple games with Franz or went for a short walk. Franz especially liked it when Ludwig pushed him high up into the air in our *Schiffschaukel*, our boat-shaped swing.

Franz loved to eat, and he could eat a lot. He was especially fond of sweets. In September, when the prune plums on our trees were ready, Mama always made lots of *Zwetschgendatschi*, a yeast sheet cake covered with lots of plums sweetened with sugar and cinnamon. The wasps liked it, too, and when Mama baked these cakes, wasps came in through the open windows and we had to hang up sticky yellow fly strips.

Mama never just baked one cake, she always baked two, they disappeared so fast. Those cakes were certainly the highlight of

Franz's Sunday visits. Sometimes he just couldn't wait any longer, and he would ask Mama if it wasn't coffeetime yet.

After coffee, my parents often played board games with us until one of Franz's brothers came to pick him up. Sometimes we sent whatever clothing Ludwig had outgrown home with them. Usually, one or the other of Franz's brothers found articles of clothing they could wear.

We became quite attached to our Sundays with Franz, partly because on those Sundays there were no long walks with our parents looking at other people's yards and plantings, and partly because gradually Franz had endeared himself to us. Franz came all that summer and fall until school started again. He had helped to make our summer a happy and eventful one, but it was also a summer that held a shocking aftermath, which we didn't realize until several years later.

It was some time in the spring of the next year that Papa saw Franz's brother after church and inquired about Franz.

"We're quite hopeful. He was sent to a special clinic for treatment. They'll check to see if anything can be done for him," he said.

"Well, we hope they can help him. Let us know how he's doing," Papa answered.

We never saw Franz again, and neither did his family. His family was later notified that he had died of natural causes and had been cremated.

Two years later, in 1941, Bishop Count Clemens von Galen's sermons publicly exposed Hitler's program to euthanize those who were physically or mentally handicapped. This program was implemented in great secrecy in 1939, and thousands of disabled children and adults were euthanized during the years 1939 to 1941—Hitler considered them "life unfit for life."

To inform the populace, several priests in Bishop von Galen's diocese printed and distributed his sermons. The shocking news spread by word of mouth from town to town, and that is how we first heard about it. My parents were horrified. This was so outrageous, they thought it must be a false rumor and did not tell me. I found out about it much later.

Bishop von Galen was put under house arrest. However, the diocesan priests who had distributed the sermons were arrested and executed.

We often wondered, was Franz one of those unlucky children? We never found out.

But what we did find was that we could not forget the Franz of those summer Sundays: The fun-loving boy whose disability did not stop him from participating in our games or wolfing down Mama's cakes.

Chapter 14

Philippe

The summer of 1939 promised to be exciting with travel and adventure, and it was—until the day the mail carrier arrived on his yellow bicycle with the telegram that so abruptly changed our lives forever.

My brother, Ludwig, had made excellent progress at the *Gymnasium* he attended in Pasing, a suburb of Munich. The *Gymnasium*, a school for gifted students, stressed academics. After he had fulfilled the requirements of Latin, old Greek, and English, he elected to study French. It was his favorite language. Forever wanting to improve his French, he often listened to French broadcasts on the radio.

A committee of professors at the *Gymnasium* selected him to be an exchange student to France during the summer of 1939. He was to spend six weeks with his host family, the Cartiers, who lived in St. Etienne with their two children, Philippe and Lisette. The Cartier's son, Philippe, would then spend six weeks in Germany with our family. Like Ludwig, Philippe was eighteen years old. Lisette was two years older.

The Cartiers also invited my parents and me to visit them in St. Etienne and to travel with them through France during a week of Ludwig's stay. On my parent's behalf, Ludwig wrote a letter to the Cartiers, thanking them and accepting their invitation. In turn, my parents invited them to visit us and to travel with us through Germany during the time of Philippe's visit.

Ludwig was ecstatic, of course, and immediately started practicing his French on us.

Mama was already in a dither, eagerly planning what foods she might prepare when Philippe would be staying with us, while Papa studied the map on where St. Etienne was, relative to the places he had been during World War I.

I, too, was excited. Excited like an 11 year old—going on 16! Just the thought of being in France sounded so romantic to me and then to visit Paris . . . I couldn't believe it was really going to happen.

It was July, and Ludwig was preparing to leave for France. To get the most out of his visit, my parents had bought him a new camera and a notebook. They reminded him to take lots of pictures and to keep a daily log.

Along with getting the necessary clothing ready, Mama also felt she had to be sure to give him all kinds of advice. She admonished him to be helpful, to be punctual, to eat what was set before him, to be honest and respectful—in other words, not to embarrass the family. After all, this was his first time for him to be on his own for a long stretch and in a foreign country at that.

On a bright sunny July day, my parents and I accompanied Ludwig to Munich and put him on the train to France. We arrived early, and Ludwig was happy to find a seat by a window. Mama urged him to write, she especially wanted to know about the foods they served, while Papa again told him to take lots of pictures. We all wished him a good trip, the whistle blew, and Ludwig was on his way to France.

We couldn't wait for his first letter. When it finally arrived, we learned that the whole Cartier family, as well as some of Philippe's classmates, had welcomed him at the train station in St. Etienne.

"I like speaking French, but it's a challenge," he wrote.

He went on to say that he was glad to have his dictionary to look up new words and phrases. Idioms, the way people speak, were the most troublesome for him, since that's not what he was taught at school. Most important was that he thought his French was improving.

Then in his letter he said, "Monsieur and Madame are very nice, and I get along fabulously with Philippe and Lisette. Philippe has introduced me to his friends from school. They all like music, and Philippe has tickets for us to see a play."

It was easy for us to read between the lines that he was fitting in well with his exchange family and loving his new experiences.

His letter continued: "Sunday dinner here takes several hours. We eat one course, drink some wine, talk and visit, eat another course, and so on. I am getting used to eating my beef rare, like they do. And every morning boys on bicycles deliver long thin sticks of crusty white bread, called baguettes. The bread sticks out on the back of their bikes. It's not wrapped or anything. Madame only buys enough bread for one day because by the next day it is hard and stale. Tomorrow, we're off to Belfort to meet Philippe's grandparents."

Finally came the day when my parents and I were on the train to St. Etienne. Customs officials boarded the train just before the border. While the train traveled on, they checked and stamped everyone's passport. At the next station, they got off the train. We were in France.

Our two families enjoyed getting to know each other, and even though I couldn't understand a word, I accompanied Madame and Lisette whenever they went shopping.

We used facial expressions and gestures to get our ideas across. Sometimes it was like a game of charades to watch all of us trying to "converse."

Mme. Cartier was always admiring my curls, so I slept in curlers and then followed up with quite a ritual every morning to get the curls looking just right, especially for Madame. I liked the outgoing and vivacious dark-haired woman with the winning smile and loved to hear her talk. Listening to her every word, I vowed to learn French as soon as I could in school.

Lisette was in nurse's training. She was her mother's daughter, happy and outgoing, while Monsieur Cartier was a rather quiet and reserved gentleman who once in a while smiled and nodded to me from behind his newspaper; that was all the reaction I got from him whenever I tried to "talk" with him.

And then there was Philippe, with his slow and irresistible smile.

Soon it was time for the Cartiers to show us a part of their country. The first city our two families visited was Paris, the "City of Lights." Everyone except Mama and I took the elevator to the top of the Eiffel Tower. I was very disappointed and let everyone know how much I wanted to go along, but Mama did not like heights and thought it might be too much for me also.

Here we are with Philippe, our French foreign exchange student, in front of the Eiffel Tower in Paris in 1938.
From left: Philippe, Mama, me, Papa, and Ludwig.

So Mama and I strolled along the beautiful flower beds at the foot of the Eiffel Tower, trying to identify the various kinds, but the waiting got to be long, and we started to get tired. Finally, we sat down on some chairs along one of the flower beds. A woman came and started talking to us. She became rather agitated when she got no reply, just the same uncomprehending little smile from both of us.

Somehow, after the woman gestured and showed us some coins, Mama realized that she wanted us to pay for the privilege of sitting on one of these chairs. Mama had no French money because Ludwig took care of our bills. Reluctantly we got up and walked around until the others came down from the Tower.

After this experience, Ludwig gave Mama a quick lesson on the value of the various French bills and coins, and Mama began to keep some small bills and change in her billfold in case she needed cash.

The Eiffel Tower adventure being over, we took advantage of the pleasant afternoon and strolled along the Seine River, checking out the offerings of the various *bouquinists,* the bookstalls that lined the river.

"Anneliese, these are for you," Philippe said as he handed me a large envelope filled with stamps. "Ludwig has told me that you are an avid stamp collector. You probably don't have these yet. Some are from the French Colonies in Africa like Nigeria, the Ivory Coast, Dahomey, and Senegal."

"Oh, my album pages of the French colonies are blank," I stammered, as I thanked him for my present.

My heart was skipping beats, and I knew my face was red, like a ripe tomato. I had developed a secret crush on Philippe, who was tall, had dark curly hair and was, after all, a real Frenchman.

I am sure now that his gift was meant to be a nice gesture for the sister of his exchange brother. But to me, at that time, it was so much more. I was going to have so much to tell my friends in school about my trip to France and especially about Philippe.

The Cartiers continued to introduce us to France by taking us to many fascinating places with historic and aesthetic interest. I didn't realize it at the time, but traveling in France at my young and impressionable age would leave me with deep and lasting memories. At the moment, it was simply a grand adventure.

Near Paris, we visited the luxurious castle of Versailles with its splendid Hall of Mirrors. Close to Verdun-sur-Meuse, we saw a half-buried, rusty helmet, which was a silent witness to one of the longest and bloodiest battles to take place during World War I.

In the village of Givenchy, Papa reflected back to January 28, 1916, when he was lying severely wounded on this battlefield.

"I didn't know your mother then, but it was on her twentieth birthday that I was wounded here," he said.

After Givenchy, we continued on to Belfort, where we met Philippe's grandparents. We had a most pleasant time with them while Ludwig and Philippe were kept busy translating.

I fondly remember that the high point of our visit was the beautiful Loire Valley.

"You need to look for cave-homes in this region," Philippe explained. "They are dug into the hillsides and only their chimneys poke out of the ground."

"Cave homes—and people still live in them?" I asked in disbelief.

"Yes, people live in them, but some are used for storing wine now. The temperature in these caves doesn't vary much. That's ideal for storing wine."

Arriving at the first castle, Ludwig translated, as Madame explained: "This region is known as the Garden of France. It has many castles and also fortresses. Here we are at Chenonceau, known as *Le Chateau des Dames,* the castle of the ladies, because the ladies living in it at various times shaped and made it what it is today."

"Oh, neat. Who were the ladies that lived in it? Were they queens?" I asked.

"Yes, several were. But one of the most interesting stories is that of Diane de Poitiers. She was King Henry II's favorite. Diane was much older than the King, very beautiful, intelligent, and influential. King Henry II gave her Chenonceau as a gift.

"After King Henry II died, the queen, Catherine de Medici, forced Diane to give up her beloved Chenonceau and move to an austere feudal fortress," explained Madame.

Madame's story about Diane de Poitiers and the castle completely fascinated and enthralled me. To an eleven-year old, it was full of mystery and romance.

A visit to the principality of Monaco and to the casino in Monte Carlo concluded the tour.

Since only adults were allowed in the casino, Mama and I again had "garden time." The flowers and gardens were beautiful, but did not appease me. I desperately wanted to see what was going on inside a real gambling casino.

Our week with the Cartier family had gone by much too fast. Soon it was off to St. Etienne for a day, and then it was time for us to say good-bye to our hosts. Ludwig was staying with the Cartiers one more week. I had become very attached to Madame and hated to leave. My parents consoled me by reminding me that Monsieur and

Mme. Cartier, along with Lisette, would come to stay with us during the time of Philippe's exchange. Then we would all tour Germany together.

Mama, Papa, and I returned home to get things ready for Ludwig and Philippe's arrival the following week. Mama did a lot of cleaning, shopping, and stocking up on food. I carefully sorted and added the new stamps to my stamp album so I could show it to Philippe.

After what seemed an eternity to me, Ludwig and Philippe arrived in Munich. Of course, I tried to tag along with them whenever possible. One day, I was looking for them when I saw two wisps of smoke on the garage roof. Upon investigation, I found Philippe and Ludwig sitting on the roof, smoking strong-smelling French cigarettes.

I am quite sure now that they were up there to get away from me for a while. Not wanting to be left out, I cajoled them into letting me have a few puffs. Soon I was quite sick.

"I don't think you'll try this again soon" was Mama's only comment to me. *I never want to try cigarettes again,* I vowed to myself.

There are many happy things I remember about Philippe's time with us. One is my recollection that Philippe was especially fond of Mama's *Rindsrouladen,* beef rollups, with bread dumplings. Whenever we had the large Bavarian dumplings, Philippe would tease us and call them cannonballs because they were so much bigger than the *boulettes* of his country.

Philippe and Ludwig had many of the same interests. They did everything together, not the least of which was to attend several operas, and, in true student fashion, they bought inexpensive student tickets and stood way up in the gallery to hear the magnificent music and marvel at the lavish costumes.

Philippe also loved to discuss politics. Unfortunately, he was not shy about voicing his opinions quite strongly. "You better not express these opinions out in public," Ludwig cautioned him.

We were aware that in one of his speeches, Hitler had proclaimed that cannons were more important than butter. Germany had been importing butter from Denmark and Holland since Germany was not producing enough butter itself. This was stopped, and steel was imported instead. That change in policy was not hard to interpret.

"I think Hitler is pushing for war," Papa commented.

"Talk like that can put all of us all in danger," Mama cautioned, and I sensed the concern in her words.

It was the last week of August. Philippe had been with us for about four weeks when the mailman arrived on his bright yellow bicycle to deliver a telegram for him.

As Philippe proceeded to read it, his expression became somber.

"I'm to return to France immediately. It says there is imminent danger of war," Philippe blurted out.

Momentarily, there was silence while everyone tried to comprehend this alarming news. I was stunned. *War? With whom? Why?* So many questions ran through my head, and it was as if something had suddenly taken away the brightness of the sun.

Papa was first to regain his composure as he explained what needed to be done.

"I'll check the train schedules and make the necessary travel arrangements," he said. "Ludwig and I will accompany Philippe to the border, or as far as we are allowed. We can't waste any time. We have to get Philippe across before they close the borders."

Turning to Ludwig, he asked him to get Philippe's suitcases from the attic and help him get packed. Mama and I fixed sandwiches, sliced cheese, and picked some of the juicy plums from our tree for them to eat. They would be able to buy beverages on the train.

Philippe promised he would come back to finish his exchange after this war was over. In everyone's opinion, if there really was going to be a war, surely it would be a short one. There were some border skirmishes with Poland in the news, but everyone hoped they would be resolved soon.

We said our sad good-byes, and Mama and I shed some tears. We all hated to see Philippe go and dreaded the thought of war.

Ludwig and Papa traveled with Philippe as far as the German border, where they got off the train and waved a last good-bye to Philippe as the train pulled out of the station and headed into France. Then Papa and Ludwig returned home on the last train, late that same night.

We were all in shock. What had been such an amicable experience for all of us had ended abruptly with fear and concern for what this war was to bring.

Eventually, we had our reunion with the Cartiers, but it turned out ever so different from the way we had imagined. It was not the happy occasion we had envisioned.

It was twelve years after the war when the Cartiers and Lisette came to visit my parents in Munich. Philippe was not with them. He had died in a concentration camp during the Occupation of France. He had voiced his political opinions too openly. We shared bittersweet memories of the Philippe we had known, and we mourned his loss. For a short time during that pleasant and unsuspecting summer so many years ago, he had been our brother.

Rindsrouladen—Beef Roll-Ups

3 pounds boneless beef sirloin steak,* cut about ¼-inch thick, trimmed of fat
German style mustard (or Grey Poupon)
Bacon slices
Dill pickles, cut in half lengthwise (quartered if they are big)
Vegetable oil
1 bay leaf
1 envelope dry onion soup
3 cups beef stock
1 cup sour cream (I use light sour cream)
4 tablespoons flour
Salt and pepper to taste
1 teaspoon instant coffee (optional)
Metal poultry skewers or strong toothpicks

1. Cut the bacon slices in half, and precook in microwave to eliminate some of the fat.
2. Thinly spread each slice of steak with mustard. Place a slice of bacon down the center. Lay a pickle on top and roll up. Fasten with toothpick or metal skewer.
3. Heat a small amount of vegetable oil in large skillet and brown the roll-ups. Place in large pot or crockpot. Add 3 cups hot beef broth, bay leaf and onion soup mix. Simmer until meat is tender.
4. When meat is tender, discard bay leaf and remove roll-ups to a warm serving dish.

Make a paste of the 4 tablespoons flour and about a cup of water and add to the liquid. Cook until gravy is thick. Add sour cream and heat through; do not boil. Add coffee (optional) to give the gravy a rich flavor. Return roll-ups to gravy and heat through.

Beef roll-ups are usually served with *Spätzle*, bread dumplings, or wide noodles. Red cabbage also goes well with beef roll-ups.

* I call the meat man a day ahead so he can cut the meat while it is frozen.

Chapter 15

War Breaks Out

I was five years old when Hitler seized power in 1933 and quickly and effectively eliminated our freedoms.

In March of that year, Hitler established Dachau, a former ammunition factory on the outskirts of Munich, as the first *Konzentrationslager*, concentration camp (KZ), for political prisoners. Thousands of Hitler's opponents were arrested and sent to Dachau almost immediately after he assumed control.

It was only much later, after the war that I—and many Germans—became cognizant of the monstrous acts committed there, of its infamy.

During 1934's Operation Hummingbird, also called the "Night of the Long Knives," Hitler eliminated members of the SA, the paramilitary brown shirts who had helped him to power, and their leader, Ernst Röhm. The SA under Röhm was becoming too independent, he thought. These murders were treated as if they had been necessary to forestall a coup. The German radio and press reported these murders as the *Röhm-Putsch*, the Röhm-Coup. The Night of the Long Knives represented a victory for Hitler. In his speech to the Reichstag on July 13, 1934, he proclaimed himself to be "the supreme judge of the German people." He, one man, had set himself above the law.

In quick succession, Hitler marched his troops into the Rhineland and annexed Austria, negating the harsh treaty of Versailles, without shedding a drop of blood. No country challenged these actions. The "Munich Treaty" of Sept. 29, 1938, signed by Neville Chamberlin, prime minister of Great Britain, and Edouard Daladier, prime minister of France, gave in to Hitler's demands, and he added the Sudetenland to his conquests.

My parents and people in Germany were relieved. War with Czechoslovakia was averted, they thought, but in March 1939, Hitler broke his promise not to make more territorial demands in Europe and marched into Czechoslovakia. Actually, by appeasing the tyrant, the diplomats had made war more inevitable.

In late August 1939, our radio and newspapers reported alleged atrocities committed against German people living along the Polish border. These atrocities actually had not been committed by the Poles but had been staged by the Nazi echelon as a propaganda device to justify the invasion of Poland.

There was much unrest and uncertainty in the neighborhood where we lived, but no one dared to speak openly against the war or against the *Führer*. People had learned to be very cautious about political remarks, even in front of their children. After all, a small child could naively repeat in public what had been said by a parent, and this could have deadly consequences.

"What you hear in these walls is not to be repeated to anyone," Mama often cautioned me.

People were so wary of being denounced that they would look over their shoulder before voicing an opinion to make sure they were not being overheard. Sometimes a person disappeared, but no one dared ask questions. If you valued your life, and the lives of your family, you did not ask too many questions in Nazi Germany.

It was in July 1934 that the *Reichsarbeitsdienst, RAD,* the compulsory labor service for young men after they turned eighteen, was established. The men of the *RAD* were pictured with a shiny spade on their shoulder. A year later, they had to trade their spade for a gun. Ludwig was almost nineteen, but since he was in his last year of study at the *Gymnasium,* his induction into the *RAD* was postponed until graduation.

On September 1, 1939, just a few days after our French exchange student, Philippe, had received the telegram calling him back to France because of impending war, German radio announced war had been declared on Poland. Mama voiced her worries about the war that had just begun. She did not want her son to become "cannon fodder" for Hitler's Army. Papa tried to reassure her.

"By the time Ludwig finishes his last year at the *Gymnasium* and then serves his stint in the *RAD*, the war will long be over," he said.

"As much as I hope that you're right, somehow I'm not convinced. Hitler wants more. His speeches sound like he's not going to be easily satisfied," Mama replied.

"Right now, let's make the most of the time Ludwig is still with us. It's Saturday night, if the kids are done with their homework, let's play *Mensch Ärgere Dich Nicht*—their favorite board game—or cards," urged Papa.

Soon we were sitting around the kitchen table. Mama went down to the vegetable cellar to bring up some of the apples from this year's harvest. Papa got out the three-tiered wooden card holder he had made to compensate for the loss of his right hand and arm. This enabled him to sort and arrange his cards without anyone's help. He was fiercely independent, even when it came to playing cards.

"Mama, will you peel my apple, please?" I pleaded. "And then put the peels on top of the stove? I like the way they smell, like baked apples."

"You're too fussy, the peelings are good for you," Ludwig chided. "You need to eat the whole apple."

"I'll peel Anneliese's apple while you deal, so let's get started."

Mama opened the drawer in the kitchen table, got out a paring knife and started peeling my apple. I loved those cozy evenings in the warm kitchen with my parents and Ludwig. I felt safe and loved.

While starting to deal the cards, Ludwig told us, "I listened to the British BBC news today. I wasn't sure I understood it correctly, so I listened to the French station, since my French is much better than my English. They accused Germany of invading Poland, not the other way around and . . ."

Papa interrupted him: "Damn it, you can't listen to those foreign stations anymore. You now get a minimum of five years in prison or even the death sentence for this. Good God, do you want all of us to go to the KZ?"

Papa pounded the table with his wooden arm, as he was prone to do when he was really angry.

"OK, OK, I'm sorry," Ludwig said. "You don't have to worry. I give you my word I'll not listen again."

Ludwig finished his last year of the *Gymnasium*, and just a few days after he was done with his exams he received notice to report for the *Reichsarbeitsdienst*. We all missed Ludwig terribly, the house felt strangely empty without him. I remember that sometimes I walked into his room to touch his things, just to feel a little closer to my brother.

Ludwig poses in his *Reichsarbeitsdienst* (RAD) uniform.

During the next year, Ludwig did hard physical labor from early morning till evening. His company had to level large rock-strewn meadows in the rolling foothills of the Alps and turn them into arable ground. All this was done by manual labor, mainly the spade.

After what seemed like an eternity to me, Ludwig finally received a weekend pass to come home. He looked so different to me when I saw him. He had lost weight, his hands were deeply calloused, and he had a dark tan from laboring outside all day. He looked and acted a lot older than the 19 year old who used to tease me before he had left just a few months earlier.

Mama was happy and thankful for every day he was at home. She always told us hard work didn't hurt anyone, but no one should have to go to war.

It was only a few days after Ludwig had completed the *RAD* that he was inducted into the Army. It was a sad day when Ludwig left. Mama took it especially hard, and I tried my best to console her.

He was assigned to a *Beobachtungsabteilung*, an observer Corps, of the army. For now, he was in training in one of the Munich garrisons. There he was instructed on how to measure the point of origin of enemy fire and report those findings back to the artillery. After a few weeks, he received his first weekend pass. For our family, it was like a holiday. And, like a holiday, those days went by too fast.

While the war with Poland was over quickly, the fighting did not stop. In April 1940, Hitler presented ultimatums to both Norway and Denmark. Denmark, a very small country to the north of Germany, gave up and became a "Protectorate" for the next four years. Norway resisted fiercely and fought bravely but was conquered in the end. In May of the same year, Hitler invaded Holland, France, and Belgium.

The war drastically changed our daily lives. The next spring, and every year during the war, our garden became larger. Papa got out the digging fork and another one of the beautiful flower beds that Mama had planted had to make way for potatoes and vegetables. Not only did my parents plant peas and beans to use fresh, they also planted extra to dry for pea and bean soup during the winter.

One corner of the vegetable cellar was partitioned off with a tall board and filled with sand. Vegetables such as carrots, potatoes, and beets kept very well in the cold sand.

Almost everything was rationed. The ration cards were different for grownups, hard laborers, expectant mothers, children, and infants. There were cards for eggs, meat, bread and flour, jam, sugar and honey, milk, oil, butter and fat, and coupons for dried peas, beans, and lentils. There was also a card for clothing. Even thread and mending cotton were rationed.

Locally grown fresh fruits and vegetables were not rationed since they would spoil. To buy fresh fruits and vegetables, it was a matter of getting to the produce market and standing in line for whatever happened to be available. Citrus fruits had to be imported from Italy and were scarce, while tropical fruits like bananas were not to be had at all.

As the war continued, food became even scarcer. It sticks in my mind that ration stamps allowed one egg per person a month. This seems unreal to me now, but that is what I remember. If one wanted, one could keep chickens, and we were allowed one-and-a-half hens per person. It was against the law to keep chickens without declaring them. If more hens were kept, the extra eggs had to be delivered to a collection place. If a hen was killed, the hen's head had to be produced as proof that no more eggs from that particular hen could be delivered.

My parents decided to get chickens to supply us with eggs and meat. Papa cleared out all of the garden tools and scrap lumber from the storage area and moved them into the garage. After all, it didn't look like we would need the garage for a car in the near future. In the empty storage area, he installed some roosts and laying boxes. He also added a fenced-in, outdoor run.

Every spring Mama would let a hen hatch out her eggs. The roosters provided some much needed meat, and the hens supplied us with more eggs than we would get with the ration card. When Mama used eggs in cooking, she always carefully wiped the egg shells out with her finger to get out the last of the egg white. We put the shells in an old pot and let them get dry and brittle. Then, whenever the pot was almost full, Mama asked me to crush the eggshells. We mixed them with the chicken feed to help the hens produce strong eggshells.

It wasn't too long after we got into the chicken business that our livestock operation expanded. Our neighbors in back were Herr and Frau Dehm and their two children, my friend Erna and her brother, Theo.

Leaning over the fence one day, Herr Dehm told Papa: "You really ought to get some rabbits. They don't take much feed, and they'll put some extra meat on your table."

115

"*Ja*, I've been thinking about that," Papa agreed. "So far, I haven't been able to get any. Would you consider selling me a pair of yours?"

"Well, you've helped me out more than once. I have a female that's been bred. You house and feed her. When the young ones are weaned, you give the female back to me with two of her offspring. That'll get you started."

"I sure appreciate that, and we'll remember you when our fruit gets ripe."

They shook hands, and we were in the rabbit business.

Papa added some rabbit hutches on the sheltered side of the garage. My job was to gather dandelion greens along the roadside for the rabbits. It was a job I didn't mind because Erna, Theo, and I usually went out together after supper, and each of us tried to be the first to fill his or her basket. The rabbits loved the dandelions, and I liked watching them eat the leaves with the milky juice running out. I didn't even mind that, after picking dandelions, my hands were always full of sticky, dark spots from the juice.

Then one day we added even more to our livestock: Papa came home with a runt piglet he had bartered for with a farmer. We hand-fed it and soon it thrived. We found room for "Susie" in the woodshed behind the garage.

My parents kept warning me not to make pets out of the animals. They were needed for food. Nevertheless, I was not happy when I came home from school on some Fridays to find one less rabbit in the cage. I didn't feel the same way about the chickens. Having chicken on Sunday was just fine with me.

Killing the animals presented a problem since Papa couldn't kill the animals with just one arm. Luckily our neighbor, Herr Soller, who, as a young man, had helped in his father's butcher shop, always killed and skinned the rabbits for us.

In exchange, he got to keep the rabbit pelts, which kept his arthritic knees warm during winter. He blamed his affliction on the cold and wet trenches of World War I. He and Papa often told us stories of their life as soldiers in the trenches and of how differently the war was fought then.

Although the animals provided us with food, we had the problem of making sure to have food for all of them to last through the winter. Papa let the grass grow tall among the fruit trees and mowed it with a scythe. It was then dried and stored in the garage to be fed to the rabbits during the winter. We also followed the radio and newspaper admonishments to feed animals only with table scraps and grains gleaned from the fields. And we saved and used for feed the outer leaves of lettuces and cabbage, beet and carrot tops, as well as potato peels.

During the grain harvest, Mama and I, along with Frau Dehm, Erna, and Theo, went to "glean" the fields almost every day. After a farmer had harvested a field, it was declared open. This meant we could go in and pick up the shafts of wheat, oats, or rye left on the ground. It was a tedious job, and we were elated if we found five or six shafts of grain the harvester had dropped in one place.

Some of the oats and rye were fed to the chickens. The wheat kernels and some of the rye and oats, however, were laboriously ground in a coffee mill for extra flour. Mama used this flour to bake bread. It was the original "multigrain" bread, with plenty of fiber, and it scratched all the way down.

During these times of rationing and short supply, our usual coffee was *Ersatzkaffee,* which was made from roasted grains and acorns, with some *Feigenkaffee,* fig extract, similar to chicory. Sometimes, however, after an especially devastating air raid, we received an extra ration of real coffee.

Before the war, we always bought whole milk. Now even our milk was changed. It had lost all of its fat content. It was blue and watery so we started calling it *blauer Heinrich,* blue Henry.

Our sugar ration was reserved for making jams, jellies, and an occasional birthday cake. To sweeten coffee, tea, or compotes made of fruit from our garden, saccharin was used.

We tried to supplement our food in any way we could. One of our favorite ways to forage was to go into the woods and look for mushrooms. On a warm spring day, after a rain, Mama packed a sack lunch, fixed a small jug with drinking water, and we started out. Often Frau Dehm, Erna, and Theo came along.

First, we took the train for a few stations, then hiked into the woods. In dense fir thickets, we looked for golden chanterelles and, among the tall trees, for a local variety called *Täuberl.* We were elated if we could add to our collection a few *Steinpilze,* boletus edulis, with their distinctive earthy smell and velvety soft brown caps.

117

I proudly showed my finds to Mama, who checked the mushrooms to make sure they were the edible kind. The day always went fast. Erna, Theo, and I competed to see who could find the most and biggest mushrooms.

At home, the mushrooms were carefully washed and sautéed with onions and lots of freshly chopped parsley. Served over bread dumplings, this dish was always a very special treat.

Mushrooms were not the only food the forest provided.

In the early spring we also picked the new outgrowth on the fir trees. Mama made *Fichtennadelhonig,* fir tree honey, from the sticky new shoots. Real honey was rationed and not easy to get. Mama combined these shoots with water and some sugar, then simmered the mixture for several hours until it thickened and was a pretty rose color. The "honey" was strained to remove the tips. Mama then put the honey in jars, sealed them, and kept them in our cool basement storeroom. It was a tasty addition to our meager rations.

There was a scarcity of most items we took for granted. During the winter of 1939 to 1940, for instance, there was a definite scarcity of coal. The next winter, the coal shortage was even worse. Even though it was prohibited, Papa sometimes went out at night to search the railroad tracks for pieces of coal dropped from the trains.

Wood also was scarce. After a storm, Papa took out our little handcart, and we headed for the forest to pick up dead branches. This was permitted by the authorities, and the forest floor was always picked clean by those of us who scavenged. It was not permitted, though, to cut down trees or cut off branches from living trees. When we were in dire need of wood, Aunt Marie, who often came along with Mama and me, had no qualms about cutting down a few bigger branches. After she cut them up, we put them on the bottom of the cart and covered them with some of the dead branches.

Not surprisingly, another commodity that was hard to get was toilet paper. It was my job to sit down with a stack of old newspapers and cut a supply of toilet paper. Before using this homemade toilet paper, however, it was necessary to crumple each sheet several times, to soften it.

There were no supermarkets, just small specialty shops. All were closed Saturday afternoons and all day Sundays. Stores also were closed for two or three hours at noontime. As one might expect, there were long lines at the dry grocers, the fruit and vegetable shop, the bakery, the butcher shop, the dairy store, everywhere.

After school, I often helped with the shopping. Mama stood in line at one shop while I joined the line at another store. Once a store had sold its supply, the rest of the people in line had to leave empty-handed.

If there was an air raid while waiting in line, we had to try again later or the next day. If the trains were bombed, the sorely needed food was either blown to bits or went up in smoke. When this happened, our ration stamps were useless. We had to go without or run the risk of the severe penalties established for people who hoarded food or sold or bought food on the black market.

One novel way to save our ration coupons was to take advantage once a month of *Eintopf Sonntag*, one-pot Sunday, at our local restaurant Spitzauer. The one-pot meal consisted of potatoes, carrots, peas, cabbage, and a few scraps of meat from Spitzauer's butcher shop. People could buy a plate of this without having to sacrifice ration stamps.

On those Sundays, my cousin Mariele and I were often required as *Jungmädel*, the Young Girls League, to help peel enormous piles of potatoes and clean vegetables for this meal. Spitzauer provided this one-pot meal, which helped us and others to conserve ration stamps, but as with all other restaurants, it was required to have two meatless meal days a week.

The war taught us in a short time that there really are very few necessities in life. What we had deemed necessities before the war were unavailable luxuries now, and we had to do without them.

Mama no longer was able to get her favorite soap, *Puhl's Garten Nelke*, or *Flieder*, Puhl's carnation- or lilac-scented soap, which used to perfume our linen closet before the war. Instead, Mama bought whatever soap was available. We no longer had the luxury to be selective.

Leberknödelsuppe—Liver Dumpling Soup

This soup is a specialty in Bavaria where it can be ordered in most restaurants. During the war, we were able to get double the amount of meat our ration coupons called for if we bought "organ meat." This nourishing soup helped stretch our ration stamps.

For the dumplings:
1 package stale rolls (I use Earth Grain French)
1½ cup warm milk
1/2 pound beef liver, chopped fine, membranes removed
1 finely chopped onion, sautéed
1/2 cup chopped fresh parsley
2 eggs
2 teaspoons dried marjoram
Dash garlic salt
Grated rind of one-half lemon
1 teaspooon salt
1/2 teaspoon pepper

For the soup:
Hot beef broth (canned or homemade)
Chopped chives, for garnish

Cut rolls into thin slices. Place in large bowl and pour warm milk over the bread. Cover and let soak for about 30 to 40 minutes. Add the liver, sautéed onion, parsley, and remaining ingredients to the bread and milk mixture. Mix well. If the mixture is too soft, add some bread crumbs.

Bring a large bowl of salted water to a boil. Dip your hands in a bowl of cold water and form dumplings. Gently lower dumplings into the boiling water. Simmer for about 20 to 25 minutes.

Put a dumpling into each soup plate and ladle hot beef broth over it. Sprinkle with chopped chives. Serve immediately.

Chapter 16

The War Expands

In the spring of 1941, our neighbor, who was allowed to have a telephone because she owned a laundry, came to our house quite excited:

"Frau Heider, Ludwig called. He told me to tell you he is on a troop train headed for Vienna. They will have a day's layover there tomorrow. Ludwig is hoping you might be able to come see him."

Mama thanked her for her kindness and then immediately got busy and baked a bundt cake that would travel well. She also packed some fruit and went to the store to get some cheese with our ration cards.

The early morning hours found Papa, Mama, and me on the train to Vienna. Ludwig's troop train had already arrived when we got there. His eyes lit up and a big grin spread across his face when he saw us. We spent some bittersweet hours visiting with him.

The soldiers had not been told their destination, but Ludwig said rumors had it that they would be deployed to one of the Balkan states, Romania or Bulgaria. My parents didn't say anything in front of Ludwig, but I could tell that they were puzzled. Why Romania? Bulgaria? Could Hitler be going to war against Russia? Surely not. After all, there was the 1939 non-aggression pact between Germany and Russia.

It was late at night when the troop train pulled out of the station. It was a difficult good-bye. When would we see Ludwig again? We were able to catch the last train back to Munich.

On June 22, 1941, Germany and the Axis forces invaded Russia with 4.5 million men in Operation Barbarossa. (By the spring of 1942, German losses reached one million men.) This added a 1,800-mile front, and we knew that my brother, Ludwig, was somewhere along this front. We all were worried about him. Sometimes, as we sat down to have a meal, Mama broke into tears, wondering where her son was and if he had anything to eat.

Whenever a special coupon for chocolate was called up on my youth ration card, I usually ate only one and asked her to send the rest to Ludwig right away so I would not be tempted to eat another one. I knew how much my brother loved chocolates. I also knew he needed them more than I did.

Ludwig's first Christmas in Russia.

Ludwig stands in a truck of the German Army's
observer corps in Russia.

The war also affected our schools. I was in seventh grade. My teacher was Herr Kaiser, a stalwart member of the SA, who often wore his brown shirt uniform to school. He carried a bamboo stick while he walked up and down between the rows of our desks. He would ask a question and, instead of calling on us by name, he quickly turned and with his bamboo stick hit the desk of the student who was to answer the question. He hit it so hard that, in my case, I was sometimes so scared that I could not have told him my name, much less answered his question. When we were addressed, we had to get up from our seat. There were many times I stood, looking at the top of my shoes, unable to speak.

Whenever the teacher entered the class, we all had to stand beside our desks. One morning, after the usual "Heil Hitler," he told me in front of the class:

"I met your father yesterday. His hair looks like it got snowed on."

What was I to do? Did he expect some kind of reply from me? I was mortified.

After what seemed an eternity to me, he told the class to be seated.

I wanted to crawl under the desk. I had never thought much about Papa's age. Eight years older than Mama, Papa had grayed very early. The only way I knew him was with a full head of wavy gray hair. This had never bothered me. In fact, I had always thought it somehow looked handsome.

But Herr Kaiser's remarks embarrassed me and made me uncomfortable. More than ever, I wished I could be in some other teacher's class.

Herr Kaiser had favorites. They were the pretty girls, not the beanpoles like my best friend, Johanna, or me. There were cliques in our class now, and Johanna and I felt like outsiders. I feared and hated Herr Kaiser.

It was then that the war actually came to my rescue. With all of the able-bodied men on the front, there was an acute shortage of workers, and the farmers in our area needed help to rid the potato fields of the harmful brown-and-yellow striped potato beetles. In order to save the crops, our entire class was marched out to the potato fields. As we walked through the rows of potato plants in bloom, we laboriously picked off the bugs, one by one.

In the fall, we were out in the potato fields again, this time for the harvest. From early in the morning until late afternoon, we picked up the potatoes that had been dug with a horse-drawn machine.

We stopped only for a simple lunch, which the farmer's wife brought out into the field. There also was a short rest break in the forenoon and in the afternoon. This went on until the harvest was completed. Our learning was put on the back burner.

Even though I was exhausted every night, working in the potato fields was a relief for me. I didn't have to face Herr Kaiser in class. Johanna and I made sure we worked one of the rows as far from him as possible. By the end of the school year, however, I had little self-esteem left. I felt like a worm without a hole to crawl into, awkward and totally unsure of myself.

Helping to bring in the harvest was not only required of our classes but also of the older students, like my cousin Mariele. Classes from her school, an all-girl private school, were taken to the Holletau area north of Munich. There, Mariele and her whole class picked hops for the breweries in Munich. This was a itchy job because the hops' vines and bracts are tough, scratchy, and sticky. At night, the girls slept on straw in one room of the farmhouse. They returned home only on weekends.

For the next school year, my teacher was Miss Miller, a no-frills, down-to-earth spinster who treated us fairly. Her "Heil Hitler" every morning was rather sloppy and short, almost as if she didn't mean it. As long as we turned in our assignments and paid attention in class, we had nothing to fear. She never once during the whole school year used physical punishment. Her bamboo stick served solely to point out places on the map or on the blackboard. Thanks to Miss Miller, I started to enjoy school again and gradually regained some confidence. Both Mama and I appreciated Miss Miller immensely.

When I found out she liked red and black currants, Mama invited her to come during the berry season to pick her own fresh berries.

One summer day, the bell at the gate rang, and there was Miss Miller. Miss Miller, Mama, and I picked currants together, shared a few laughs and had a good time. I was surprised how easy it was for me to talk with my teacher. My experience with Miss Miller in the classroom, and while berry picking, gave me back my desire to go on with my schooling.

I took and passed the entrance examination for a private business and liberal arts school. Other students in my class became apprentices and attended vocational school several afternoons a week. And so our daily lives and my education continued.

My time outside of school, homework, and the required *Jungmädel*, Young Girls League, meetings was taken up with various activities made necessary by the war.

That fall Mama and I were required to complete a first aid course. During and after Allied air raids, we could not rely on ambulances or medical personal to help us. They simply were not available. If we were injured, we had to rely on our own skills. We learned about the pressure points to keep people from bleeding to death, how to apply a tourniquet, how to bandage different types of wounds, how to make emergency splints and other first aid techniques.

We also spent hours rolling bandages for the front. Working with the first aid mannequins made me think of my dolls. It was not so long ago that I played with them. These "dolls" were supposed to teach me how to save lives.

We were issued gas masks and learned how to use them. I hated the gas masks. They were uncomfortably tight on my head and smelled so strongly of rubber that it made me gag. When we had to practice walking around while wearing them, I could only do that when I cheated and put a pencil stub in the side of my gas mask, right above my ear, to feel less constricted and to maybe breathe some fresh air.

Aside from the extra burdens the war necessitated, even the everyday activities we had taken for granted became cumbersome. On the rare occasion Mama or I went to the beauty shop, we now had to bring our own towel as well as wood to heat the water.

Permanents in those days were quite an ordeal. I still remember my first perm. After the shampoo, my hair was rolled up in heavy metal curlers and doused with the most putrid smelling liquid. My head became even heavier after clamps were put over the curlers to connect them with electric cords to the permanent machine. Finally the beautician put cotton under the curlers on my forehead and all around to keep the skin from getting burned. The machine was turned on. When some spots of my scalp became too hot, the beautician handed me a fan to cool the area. Nevertheless, the next day I had several burned spots on my scalp. I didn't have another perm for a long time because of the ordeal the first one had been and because, as the war continued and air raids became more frequent, there were no more perms or trips to the beauty parlor.

Something as simple as bath time at our house became regimented. My aunt and uncle's house was built later than our house and had a furnace that heated the water. Since rationing provided only enough wood and coal for the kitchen cook stove, their furnace was useless. They no longer could take hot baths at their house.

We didn't have a furnace. Instead, we had a hammered brass water heater, with a firebox underneath it, in the bathroom. We could simply fire up our bathroom water heater with extra wood gleaned from the forest for baths. We invited the Rieflers to bring a few pieces of wood to keep the water hot and take their baths at our house.

Saturdays, after we had our baths, I ran to the Rieflers to let them know that the bathroom was ready for them. They would arrive with their wood, towels, and clean clothes. Although we didn't know it at the time, we were acquiring good practice because two years later our baths really had to run on a tight schedule as even more people depended on our bathroom.

In the evenings at home, we knit socks, mittens, scarves, and pulse warmers to send to Ludwig in Russia. In our *Jungmädel* meetings, we also knit items to be sent to soldiers in Russia.

We also made our own house slippers from scraps of felt and heavy material. Aunt Marie got us the pattern and mold to shape them. When we were through with them, Aunt Marie picked up the pattern and mold and passed them on to the next family. The sole was sewn on by using an awl to make the holes in the heavy fabric, so we could pull the needle through with the heavy *Zwirn,* thread.

In summer we were able to buy sandals made of wooden soles, which were in sections so they could bend with the foot. The uppers were heavy canvas-type material strips. These shoes were anything but comfortable. But they were available, so we wore them.

Wanting and needing some new things to wear made us inventive.

Johanna and I had seen tops that were knit from narrow gauze bandages that had been dyed. We were in the midst of fashioning our own, when this was found out and it was *streng verboten,* absolutely forbidden, to do this.

Sometimes help came when we least expected it.

One Sunday afternoon Aunt Therese and Uncle Georg arrived. Uncle Georg carried a rather bulky bag, which he put on the table. Aunt Therese explained:

"I noticed that Anneliese needs a winter coat. She really has shot up. This is one of mine. You can have it redone for her."

Saying this, she pulled a dark blue coat out of the bag.

"Oh, you've answered my prayer. She needs a coat badly, but can you spare it?"

"I do have two other coats . . . bought them before the war. Anneliese really needs this one more than I do."

I was overjoyed. I hated going to school in a coat that was already too short last year.

Aunt Therese and Uncle Georg had no children. Aunt Therese was able to buy many nice clothes before the war. Mama and I took the coat apart seam by seam, washed it and turned the material before taking it to our seamstress. That winter, I had a warm new winter coat.

Another unexpected find was when Mama cleaned the attic. The flag of the Kingdom of Bavaria was a pretty blue, like the Bavarian sky. But we could no longer fly it. We had to fly the swastika.

That gave Mama an idea. On all of my dresses, the hems had been let out and even added on to. So Mama decided that in that flag was just enough material to have a *dirndl* made for me. When the dress was finished, Mama took some white embroidery thread and embroidered around the neckline and the hem.

With a white blouse underneath it made a nice school dress for me, and I loved my *"Fahnenstoff Dirndl,"* flag *dirndl.* Since my *dirndl* was such a success, Mama took one of her extra half linen sheets and had a full skirt and fitted top made for me.

I embroidered the top and several places around the skirt bottom with bouquets of the flowers of our Bavarian Alps, the blue gentian, the alpine rose, and the Edelweiss, and had a nice outfit to wear all summer.

Mama was busy all day, trying to put food on the table, and, even in the evenings, she didn't rest. Her evenings were spent mending, darning, or knitting. When every place on the bottom and toe part of Papa's socks had been darned, Mama cut off the bottoms and knit new bottoms onto the cuff. If our stockings had a run, we used a stocking hook and laboriously reattached the runs.

On December 7, 1941, the Japanese bombed Pearl Harbor, and four days later Hitler declared war on the United States. We couldn't believe it. It seemed we were fighting the whole world.

I thought of my grandmother in New York, Aunt Katherine, Uncle Joe, and the other relatives. We knew they were safe, but we missed hearing from them, and we knew that they were worried about us.

And now it was Christmas of 1941 and still no end of the war. In former years, our Christmas tree reached from the floor to the ceiling. Because of the fire danger in case of air raids, our tree this year was small enough to stand on a small table. It had some decorations but no candles.

Aunt Marie, Uncle Willie, and Mariele came to spend a quiet Christmas with us. We missed Ludwig more than ever. I tried to take his place at the piano and played some Christmas songs, but deep down our hearts were sad. I think we all were glad when the holidays were over, and the new year came. Would it bring an end to the war?

When my 14th birthday came, Mama surprised me with a wonderful looking *Torte*, a multilayered cake. Before the war, Ludwig and I always had been allowed to choose the menu for our birthday dinner. Since the war started we were happy to just have something to eat. A real *Torte* was the utmost luxury.

A new recipe, it was called *Wassertorte*, Water *Torte*, because it used hot water and eggs, which we had, thanks to our chickens. It required no fat, which we did not have. The layers were filled with Mama's quince jelly, and the only decoration was a light sifting of confectioner's sugar, sifted over the cake through a paper doily, which gave it a beautiful lacy appearance. Each slice was a wonderful treat and made me feel special in spite of the war.

I still love quince jelly and buy it whenever I can find it.

Chapter 17

The *Pflichtjahr*, Women's Duty Year

While we carried on the best we could with our daily lives, there always hung over us fear and anxiety, mainly for Ludwig, who was on the front in Russia. His safety was constantly on our minds and in our prayers.

Then, to make matters worse, my cousin Mariele, 16 years old, had to report for her *Pflichtjahr*.

The *Pflichtjahr*—duty year—or *Landjahr*—country year—was the women's equivalent to the men's *Arbeitsdienst*. As soon as girls finished their schooling, they had to spend one year working where there was a need. It might be on a farm or in a family with several children, where the father was at the front, or in an ammunitions factory.

Naturally, the uncertainty of where Mariele would be sent, and what kind of life she would have for a year away from her family. added to our concerns. I was bereft. First, my only brother was in the army and in harm's way, and now my cousin Mariele was to go off for a year to some unknown circumstance.

Mariele hoped that she would not be assigned to an ammunitions factory and was relieved when she found out she would work on a large farm in the beautiful Eifel region. Located in western Germany, the Eifel is a low mountain range and is bordered by the Moselle River in the south and the Rhine River in the east.

From April 1941 to April 1942, she worked on this farm. I missed my brother terribly and now my cousin, too, was gone.

The farm family consisted of the farmer, his wife, and their two lively little boys. Aunt Hanna, a spinster, and Aunt Traudl, who was in her 30s and had a paralyzed leg from polio, made up part of the extended family.

Aunt Traudl was a very capable seamstress and earned her living that way. She was very kind to Mariele and taught her how to sew. A hired man, and a French prisoner of war, Julien, also worked on the farm.

While the hired man lived on the farm, Julien stayed at the POW camp. A guard marched him over from the camp early every morning and returned him to the camp after supper in the evening.

We learned later that in the confusion of the last war year Julien was able to escape and make his way back to Paris. He sent a card to the other POWS to let them know that he had been successful in getting home.

Even though she was willing to learn, it was not easy for Mariele, a city girl, to get used to life and work on a farm. Unlike the room she had at home, on the farm she had a very small room, with just enough space for a bed and a dresser. Her daily schedule was also greatly changed. She had to get up at 5 a.m. to milk the farmer's three cows. In one of her first letters home, she wrote:

"I learned how to milk the cows. Not a bad job because the stall is the only place besides the kitchen where it is always cozy and warm in winter. After I am done with the milking, I feed the pigs and the chickens. Later I take the little boys with me, and they help me gather the eggs."

In later letters, she also told us that she worked in the vegetable garden and in the fields picking potatoes, pulling sugar beets, making hay, and performing whatever work the season had in store.

Mariele told us that she cringed whenever they butchered a pig. She was glad that she was not required to help, but since she usually could hear the pig squeal, it really upset her.

When they were out working in the fields, the farmer's wife brought them the noon meal and hot coffee. Otherwise, the family, the hired hand, and the POW ate together, seated around the big kitchen table.

Sometimes they had *gestöckelte Milch*, soured milk. It was served in a big bowl placed in the center of the table and everyone dipped their fried potatoes into the milk. Simple food, but on the farm, there was enough for everyone.

Working in the barn, the fields, and in the garden was not Mariele's only responsibilities. She also helped take care of the children. On Saturdays, in addition to her usual chores, Mariele had to clean the lane from their farm to the neighbor's farm with a *Reisigbesen,* a brushwood broom. Sunday mornings, she was up early again to clean the family's and the hired man's shoes before it was time to go to church.

Since the family did not require her to go to church with them and she was tired, she always went back to bed for a few hours of much-needed sleep. Her only free time was a few hours on Sunday afternoon after the noon dishes were done until it was time for the evening chores. For all this, she received no pay, only a small allowance.

In spite of what were unusual circumstances in Mariele's world, she couldn't escape being a sixteen-year-old girl nor having the interests of a teenager. She welcomed the friendship of the young people her age in the village, and particularly that of a boy named Anton. Anton was also sixteen and the son of a neighboring farmer, a widower.

On Sunday afternoons, the only time Mariele had free, she and Anton would go for long walks through the wooded hills. Even though Mariele considered him only a friend, the young people of the village strew sawdust from his house to the farmhouse where Mariele lived. This was a custom to indicate that a couple was dating.

Anton's father would have liked to have seen his son date Mariele, but the relationship never got that far. After Mariele returned to Munich, Anton came to visit her. Mariele was glad to see him but was not interested in becoming a farmer's wife.

Anton realized that he did not fit in her lifestyle and that Mariele was not interested in him romantically, and so he returned home. They parted as friends and wrote each other for some time. Anton later married one of the local girls.

It was a great day for me when Mariele was finished with her *Pflichtjahr,* and I finally had my cousin back. However, I dreaded the time when I would have to do my *Pflichtjahr* and listened intently to everything Mariele told me about her year in the Eifel region to try and quell my anxiety.

Chapter 18

The Bunker

Reichsmarschall Herman Goering, head of the *Luftwaffe,* Air Force, had boasted in 1939 in his address to the *Luftwaffe,* that if even one enemy bomber were to reach the Ruhr, his name would not be Goering, that people could call him Meier.

These words came back to haunt him. Almost daily we read about bombings of cities along the Rhine and in the Ruhr valley. The Americans usually flew their missions in the daytime, the British at night.

So far Munich had been spared those devastating air raids. While the number of alarms increased, the actual air raids were short or in other towns. But we knew we needed to be ready for the time when we would be the target. The bombs did not discriminate. They fell on Nazis and on those who were against the regime. They fell on men, women and children alike.

So we set about preparing our basement as a shelter and put into place a plan to be followed when the air raid siren sounded. To guard our basement windows from flying shrapnel, incendiary bombs, and other debris, we had protected them with heavy cement blocks. Suitcases, packed with the most important things, stood ready to be taken to the basement as soon as the alarm sounded.

There, we immediately turned on our radio to listen to the *Luftlagemeldung,* the report that told us the area the enemy aircraft were approaching, their present position, and strength. It helped Mama to keep busy, so while waiting for the all clear, Mama and I usually took turns grinding grains we had gleaned from the fields in an old coffee grinder.

On clear nights, air raids had become a certainty, and my friends and I did homework only for the subjects we had after ten the next morning. If there was an alarm, even if it was short, school would start late, omitting the first two subjects. Typical kids, we were opportunists. We tried to find some advantage even under the worst of circumstances.

Our house was located just a few blocks, as the bird flies, from the Dornier Aircraft Factory where the night fighter planes, Do 215, and heavy bombers, Do 217, were built. We knew sooner or later we would become the target of a major air raid because of the close proximity of the aircraft factory. We just did not know when.

We were reminded every morning, and again in the evening, of how close we lived to the Dornier factory as armed guards marched forced Russian laborers past our house. A major segment of the workforce in the Dornier factory was these workers. Some of them were very young. They reminded Mama of Ludwig.

This year we had a bumper crop of fruit from our trees, and Mama shared the fruit not only with the neighbors, but she also sent Papa out with a bucket of fruit for the forced workers.

"Maybe somewhere, someone will do a good deed for our son, wherever he is," Mama said. Papa took the bucket and headed out through the garden gate.

"You there! Stand back! What do you think you're doing?" a very young guard yelled at Papa.

"Look here, son. See this wooden arm, and what used to be my hand. This is my souvenir from World War I, when you weren't even out of diapers—no, you weren't even born yet."

The guard stared at Papa's wooden arm and didn't know what to say.

"Here, have some of these pears," Papa said, offering him a few pears, then continued: "Never mind me giving *them* some," nodding to the Russian laborers. "They'll be able to work better."

Clearly confused, the guard took the pear, mumbled something, and walked on. Papa had a satisfied smile on his face as he handed out the extra fruit. He gave the empty bucket to Mama, who had been observing the whole scene from inside the garden gate. Papa got by with talking back to the guard and handing out the fruit since he was a disabled veteran. Anyone else would have been in trouble.

After that incident Papa and the guard greeted each other, and Papa had no trouble handing out any extra fruit we had.

Then came the night we had feared—our first deadly air raid. It was a clear night. The air raid sirens instantly jerked us awake, even from the deepest sleep.

There was time only to hastily pull on the clothes laid out near the bed, grab the packed suitcases, the food and water, and head for the basement.

Once we were in the basement, Papa opened the basement door to see what was going on, and I, too, wanted to see. Long fingers of light were crisscrossing the sky, searching for enemy planes above the blacked-out city. It had a scary and deadly beauty.

The drone of the bombers was louder now, and the staccato of the Flak anti-aircraft guns, echoed through the clear night. Papa hastily pushed me inside, and we joined Mama in the basement hallway.

We heard the whistling and then the ear-splitting detonation of the first bombs. The ground shook. Doors and windows slammed against their frames. We had released the locks on the windows and doors and left them ajar so they could swing back and forth and not be blown out by the blast.

The stench of the explosives began to fill the air.

Although the air raid seemed to last for hours, only a short time had passed, but it told us we were now also on the target list. The war had come to us.

The next morning, I was shocked and saddened to hear that one of my former classmates, Klara, and her whole family had perished. They lived just a few streets west of the Dornier factory. Their house had taken a direct hit.

Other houses also were destroyed, some burying the inhabitants underneath the rubble.

My Aunt Marie, while accompanying an air raid warden, heard some faint knocking coming from a pile of debris. It had been the house where some Polish women lived. They had been brought to Germany to do forced labor.

Aunt Marie immediately worked to get enough people together to dig them out. After the war, during the denazification trials, these women testified to this and other good deeds Aunt Marie had done on their behalf.

With the attacks increasing and with the limited manpower, it was difficult to get all of the people dug out before there was another air raid.

In order to avoid being buried alive by the rubble of our house, Papa and our neighbor, Herr Hager, decided to build a joint *Bunker*, air raid shelter, between our properties.

A section of the fence was taken out and the ground on each side of the fence was excavated. It was back-breaking work for the two men. The bunker was dug deep into the ground, braced with heavy timbers on the sides and railroad ties on top. How Papa was able to get old railroad ties during the war is still a puzzle to me, but he did. Several feet of sand were placed on top to extinguish incendiary bombs. There were two entrances, one for the Hagers from their property and one for us from our side. We stocked the bunker with first aid equipment, water, flashlights, candles, and non-perishable food. There was no heat in the bunker so we also kept old blankets on the benches and put rag rugs on the floor.

Whenever the alarm sounded, Papa and I took the already packed suitcases and headed for the shelter. Mama always brought any available food.

I remember the time Mama brought a paper bag with *Semmel*, hard rolls, to the bunker. I loved hard rolls and, being hungry, I convinced her that we should eat them now. After all, we might not be alive tomorrow. It worked. When the all clear sounded, I went to bed no longer hungry. Of course, we were short of rolls for breakfast.

By now, the war engulfed everything and everybody. Civilians were as likely to die a sudden violent death as the soldiers on the front. Even our chickens had become conditioned. When the air raid sirens sounded in the daytime, they automatically ran for their lives to get into the coop.

Chapter 19

Our Life is Like a Crazy Quilt

Although we tried to live our life as normally as possible during the war, it was impossible to do so.

We could maintain little order or design in our existence because of the uncertainties and the constant need to adapt to the new circumstances the war brought with it. It was as if our life was a crazy quilt with stitches going in many directions, some creating a pleasant design, others ending abruptly and often completely altered from what had been the beginnings of an apparent pattern.

Memories of the winter of 1942-43 come flooding back to me as I reflect about this crazy quilt existence.

It was that winter when, for my Christmas present, my parents gave me permission to go on a short skiing trip with my friends Johanna, Erna, and Luise. My parents had made arrangements with their friends, the Hofers, for us to stay with them at their ski lodge. It was to be a very special treat because, living in Munich, at the foothills of the Alps, we learned to ski at a young age, and we loved to go downhill skiing.

Early one morning, we took the train for the short ride to Garmisch. From there, it was a long climb up to the ski lodge. The mountains looked majestic and pristine in their coat of fresh-fallen snow. It was deceptively peaceful. The war and the destruction seemed so far removed that it could not touch us.

Here I am, ready to go skiing.

I had not seen the Hofers for several years, but they welcomed us warmly. Frau Hofer showed us to our lodging, and we hurried to get in some skiing before it got dark, letting the unpacking go until after the evening meal.

The next day, the snow was great, and we headed for the slopes shortly after breakfast. The wind was blowing in our faces, and the snow-covered landscape was a blur as we shot down the mountain. After this exhilarating experience, it was a long trek back up. There was no ski lift.

After the evening meal, we sat around the wood-burning stove in the common room, the only heated room of the lodge. Mr. Hofer brought out his accordion, and we all joined in singing some of the old mountain songs about the Edelweiss, the mountain meadows abloom with blue gentian, and about love.

After spending the day out on the blustery slopes, the warmth in the room made us tired, so we decided to turn in. We wanted to have an early breakfast again and get out on the slopes. One more day of skiing and then it would be time to return home.

We had just said our good-nights when someone came in and yelled that there was an air raid on Munich. Everyone rushed outside. We stood in the silence of the white mountains and snow-covered fir trees.

From afar, the bombing seemed like a gigantic fireworks display, but we knew better. All we could do was watch in stunned silence. We were far away from the spine-chilling whistling of the bombs and the horrendous noise of the detonation, but we were terrified, impotent to do anything.

Unable to tell what parts of Munich were being bombed, we all had the same torturing questions: *Is my family all right? Do they still have a roof over their heads?*

Since only businesses had telephones, we could not call home. We had lost all desire to stay and ski the next day. Our only thought was to get home as quickly as possible to be with our families.

Early the next morning we said our good-byes and thanked the Hofers. We skied down the mountain to the train station and were able to take the first train back to Munich.

People on the train told us about the areas of Munich where the air raid had caused the most damage. They had not heard about any damage or attack on the Dornier Aircraft factory near my parents' house.

We didn't have to say it, but my friends and I realized that this had been our last ski outing for a long time. When we finally got off the train, we put on our backpacks, shouldered our skis and parted to walk to our individual homes.

I rang the doorbell. When Mama opened the door, I realized something was different. Mama, who had not smiled much lately, couldn't hide a smile. She almost looked radiant. What had happened?

Opening the kitchen door, I saw a bowl of quince compote on the table and three small glass bowls. Compote was saved for special occasions. I also smelled "real coffee." After heavy air raids, we sometimes were issued a small amount of real coffee. Mama ground only a few beans to add to the *Ersatzkaffee* to relish those special occasions.

I looked at Mama and at Papa with surprise. They didn't know that I was coming home early. Who was the third person the dish was set out for?

"What's going on? . . . I know! Ludwig is home, isn't he? Why else would you have dessert and real coffee when it isn't a holiday?" I yelled excitedly.

Just then Ludwig stepped out from behind the door where he had been hiding. It was the most wonderful surprise for me to see my brother.

Ludwig's unit had suffered severe losses on the Russian front and was regrouping in Munich, its home base. Without Ludwig saying anything about it, we knew that they had been in the midst of heavy fighting. The days of his leave were bittersweet and rushing by much too fast. The fact that he soon would have to return to the Russian front cast a dark cloud over the joy of having him home.

Mama deplored the fact that she never knew where Ludwig was when the radio reported fighting going on in certain areas along the Russian front. Ludwig wanted to ease Mama's anguish in some way. I learned much later how he accomplished that.

Apparently, a couple of days before he had to leave again, Ludwig came into the kitchen, where Mama had just finished putting away the dishes from the noon meal and said:

"I have figured out a way for you to know where I am when I'm back in Russia. I've divided these two identical maps of Russia into eight rectangles each and numbered them from one to eight. Notice, they are the size of a regular *Feldpost*, mail to the front, envelope."

Ludwig gave one set to Mama, then continued, "When I'm back in Russia, I'll number my letters from one to eight. Then I'll put the corresponding rectangle over my envelope and stick a pin through the place on the map where my unit is located. When you get my letter, let's say it's number 5, take your rectangle number five, place my envelope over it, insert a pin where you see a tiny pinhole, and you'll know where my unit is located. No one can know about this. It must be our secret."

"Oh, Ludwig, this is great. Now at least I'll know where you are. I won't tell anyone. How did you ever think of this?" Mama cried in awe.

When Ludwig was back on the Russian front, Mama always seemed to know whether he was in a fighting area or not. During the siege of Stalingrad, Mama seemed sure that Ludwig was not there. I often asked Mama how she knew where Ludwig was. She never told me. She kept their secret until the end of the war. It was only then that she revealed all the circumstances of the plan hatched in the kitchen years before.

A few months after Ludwig returned to the front in Russia, life in our house was to change drastically.

The Allied Powers had decided in January of 1943 to intensify the bombing of German cities. Hamburg was the third largest city in Germany and an important seaport. In July 1943, the British Royal Air Force and the U.S. Army Air Force coordinated a bombing campaign against Hamburg.

In Operation Gomorrah, they bombed Hamburg around the clock for four consecutive days and nights. There were several new "firsts" in the devastation of Hamburg.

It was the first time the British Royal Air Force and the U.S. Army Air Force coordinated their bombing strikes—the Americans flying by day, the British by night.

For the first time, radar was used by the Allies to locate the targets. Advance planes dropped target indicator bombs. The bombers simply had to fly toward the slowly descending flares and drop their bombs.

For lack of a better word, we called these red or green flares "Christmas trees." They created an artificial landscape. The night was bright as day. One could read a newspaper without any trouble, even though the city was in a total blackout.

The words Christmas tree, once a symbol of Peace on Earth, Good Will to Men, now had a new sinister meaning: death and destruction from the sky.

Another new twist in the air war came in the form of aluminum tapes. Masses of these aluminum strips were dropped from planes to render the radar of the German anti-aircraft cannons useless. They also confused the German fighter planes, which found themselves attacking these "windows," as they were called, instead of the enemy aircraft.

On July 27, the RAF attacked Hamburg with more than 700 bombers, resulting in the first firestorm of the war. Temperatures of 1,800 degrees melted the asphalt in the streets and incinerated people in underground shelters to fine ashes.

After the around-the-clock bombing was over, between 40,000 and 50,000 civilians were dead, and more than one million were homeless. Fifty-five ships in the harbor were destroyed.

Many of Hamburg's homeless were housed in Bavaria. Our house, too, was inventoried, and we were informed that we could keep only the kitchen and two bedrooms for our use.

In order not to have to give up our living room, it became my bedroom. I liked the big room with all of the books and the big desk, even though now my wardrobe was also crowded into it. The living room sofa became my bed.

Baroness B. and her daughter, refugees from Hamburg, were assigned two rooms in our house. My room became their bedroom, and Ludwig's room was their living room and kitchen. They cooked their food on a two-burner hotplate.

The upstairs bathroom had to be shared and baths scheduled, on Saturdays, for them, for us, and for Aunt Marie, Uncle Willie, and my cousin Mariele.

On Saturdays, Papa would fire up the firebox beneath the brass water heater in our bathroom. In the afternoon, Aunt Marie, Uncle Willie, and Mariele came with their towels and some wood to take their baths.

The downstairs bedroom in our home had been assigned to a single woman, Fräulein Kern, who worked for the railroad in Munich. Every Friday night and again early on Monday morning she spent several hours on the train to be home with her parents and younger siblings for the weekends. For us, this was a bonus. It meant one less person in our hectic Saturday bath schedule.

The baroness and her daughter, who, before the war, had depended on servants to do their cooking, shopping, and cleaning, now often knocked on our kitchen door to question Mama about cooking or cleaning.

Both the baroness and her daughter wore beautiful jewelry. I had never seen real jewels of that size and beauty before. Sadly, it was the only thing they had left, and they wore their jewelry every day and even to the air raid bunker, which became another area that had to accommodate more people.

Mama and Papa were very generous in sharing extra fruit and vegetables from our garden, not always with good results.

Papa came home from work one day and found the bathroom toilet clogged up and running over. It was a terrible mess, and Papa worked until past midnight to get it unplugged.

Papa was irate when he found out that, instead of asking where to put potato peelings, the baroness had simply flushed them down the toilet. With all the air raids, Papa often did not get enough sleep as it was. And having to give up his sleep for unplugging the toilet did not make him happy.

Mama subscribed the incident to their lack of experience and decided she needed to take them under her wing and "educate" them. But Papa thought it was about time "they learned to do for themselves." And, gradually, they did.

Looking back, I realize that a great deal happened that constantly necessitated adjustments to our precarious lives. What had started out as a fun ski trip had ended abruptly in a hasty trip home, where the best surprise possible awaited me. My brother was home and, for a short time, I felt like we were a family again.

Then the bombings changed our lives once more as our house became a refuge for people who had lost everything.

With so many people coming and going at different times, our once private and comfortable home had become very crowded, more like a boardinghouse. Our living room, now my bedroom, became my only refuge, a place where I could withdraw from the external turmoil of our crazy quilt existence and live wherever my books and my imagination would take me.

Quittenkompott—Quince Sauce

There are quince pears and quince apples. The fruit is very hard and cannot be eaten raw. Either can be used for sauce or jelly.

2 pounds quince
2 cups water
1/4 cup sugar (or to taste)

Wash and scrub quinces thoroughly. Peel the quinces, quarter and slice them and remove the seeds. Put quince slices, along with the peel and seeds, in pan with the water and sugar. (The peel and seeds give a nice color and good flavor.) Bring to a boil and simmer until quinces are soft. Remove from heat and chill.

When serving, arrange quince slices in glass compote dishes and strain sauce over them.

Chapter 20

A Long Way Home

In March of 1944, I graduated from the business and liberal arts school I had attended and was hired by the Railroad Administration Offices in Munich, where my dad also worked. I was 16 years old.

This is my graduation photo, just before I went to work for the Railroad Administration Offices in Munich.

This is my *Arbeitsbuch*. Everyone had to have
one of these booklets to show they were employed.

Being employed by an industry important for the war released
me from serving the dreaded *Pflichtjahr*, the mandatory work service
for young women.

The office building where Papa and I worked formed a huge
square, each side a block long, with a large central courtyard. It
was located diagonally from Munich's main railroad station and
marshalling yards, a strategic and dangerous location during air
raids.

The secretarial pool where I worked was on the fourth floor with
the number of secretarial trainees fluctuating between forty and fifty.
Introductory training sessions acquainted us with the rules we were
to adhere to.

Paper was not to be wasted. If we made a mistake while typing,
we erased it, even with three or four copies. If working on a spirit
master, we had to cut out the wrong letters with a razor blade, type
the correct letters on a spare spirit master, which was kept on hand
for that purpose. The correct letters were then taped in.

The spirit masters of some of the new girls looked more like lace
doilies than the master of an official business communication.

During the cold season of the year, we wore *Pulsewärmer*, woolen
knit wristlets, to warm our wrist joints. Paper cuffs over the sleeves

of blouses and dresses kept them clean longer, thus saving precious soap powder.

I became acquainted with many of the girls in the secretarial pool. Two of them, Martina and Friedl, became my good friends.

Martina, a lively dishwater blonde, was a little more than a year older than I. She really livened up the place. The three of us ate our lunch together whenever we could, after which Martina never failed to carefully powder her nose and face before going back to work.

Friedl and I used to tease her about her old powder puff and told her it was long overdue for replacement. Unfortunately, a commodity unnecessary for the war, like a powder puff, was not easy to find.

The three of us enjoyed going to the movies together and, of course, we talked about boys and dances and dating. Our lives were void of festivity. Talking and dreaming were all we could do. There were no young men to date. They were being drafted younger and younger, and public dances had been prohibited several years ago.

In spite of, or because of, the war, we were hungry for life, and we laughed. After all, laughing was about the only thing that was not rationed. I told my friends about Herbert, who was my age and lived next door to me with his parents and his younger brother.

"Herbert used to walk with me to the train depot . . . . We both went to school in Pasing. The other kids used to tease us—told us we were sweet on each other."

"So did he kiss you?" Martina wanted to know.

"We never got the chance. One time we tried to go to the movies together, but our parents told us we were too young."

"Is he still going to the *Gymnasium?*" Friedl questioned.

"No, they drafted him right out of school, didn't allow him to finish."

"Talking about movies, let's go see *Die Feuerzangenbowle* ("The Punch Bowl") with Heinz Rühmann tomorrow night," Martina suggested. "He is so funny. The weather is supposed to be bad. We won't get caught in an air raid."

Martina was right. On a clear day or night, we could almost count on having an air raid. It was best to go out when the weather was bad. The weather during the week of July 17 had been great, and in the space of four days, large forces carried out four major strikes on Munich.

At work, in briefings about procedures during air raids, we had been instructed to always use the stairs, never the elevators. We also were required to carry our typewriters from the fourth floor to the basement air raid shelters. Typewriters were hard to replace.

The girls working on train schedules had typewriters with a wide carriage, which made them quite heavy and awkward to carry. I felt lucky to be responsible only for a typewriter with a regular carriage.

It had been over six months since I started to work in this office, and I was more at ease with the office procedure. I felt more confident that I would be able to handle new challenges each day would bring.

Wednesday, October 4, 1944, had dawned to be a beautiful clear day, so no one in our office was surprised when the air raid sirens sounded shortly before noon.

I piled my sweater, sack lunch, and purse on my typewriter, and then Martina, Friedl, and I joined the crowd heading down the stairs to the air raid shelter. In the shelter, we put our typewriters under one of the benches and sat down. By now, it was past our usual lunchtime, so we proceeded to eat our sack lunches. We had just finished eating and were visiting, typical girl-talk, when the all clear sounded. We took our time trudging back up to the fourth floor. Only now those metal typewriters felt twice as heavy and awkward as on the way down.

Scarcely had we gotten back to our work than the air raid sirens started their unnerving howl again.

My friends and I were on the crowded stairs. On each floor more people joined the mass exodus to the basement shelters. It was a challenge to keep my balance while I walked down each step, carrying the typewriter, squeezed in among the crowd.

After we arrived in the shelter, we again stashed our typewriters and sat down. Almost immediately, we heard the familiar whistling noise and the deafening detonation of bombs not too far away. Even though the whistling was intimidating and went through our very beings, we knew those were not the bombs that would kill us. The bomb that would kill us, we would not hear.

People were still on the stairs and the heavy doors to our shelter had not yet been closed when a bomb hit our staircase. Concrete dust filled the air and rubble blocked the entrance. There were the awful moans and piercing screams of the injured and dying. The smell of blood, death, and fear filled the shelter.

The air became unbreathable. Coughing and choking, we moistened our handkerchiefs with water stored in the shelter and covered our noses and mouths to filter out some of the dust. More bombs fell, accompanied always by the frantic barking of the Flak anti-aircraft cannons. The bombs virtually rained down.

Saturation bombing . . . we are the targets. What an irony. Most of my relatives on my mother's side are in America. Is one of my relatives a pilot or gunner on one of these aircraft?

Somewhere nearby someone started to pray. But my friends and I could only cling to each other in sheer panic. We were unable to stop our teeth and our bodies from shaking.

This must be how a hunted animal feels when it's cornered and knows it can't get away . . . . We are the hunted animal. We can't run away from this, we're trapped . . . . Papa is in this building, too. Oh, dear God . . . I hope he was not on the stairs. Please, God, let him be all right.

Our building took several hits and every time a bomb hit, the building shook violently. There were frantic calls for medics and for men to help extinguish incendiary bombs on the top floor. And always the whistling and then the menacing shaking when a bomb hit its target. We looked up at the ceiling, not wanting to voice our fears.

Is the ceiling going to hold, or is this whole building going to bury us alive? . . . I want out . . . let me out . . . I'd rather die out in the open . . . .

After what seemed an eternity, the all clear sounded. Our stairway was completely blocked with debris. No possibility to get out that way. The air raid shelters within the vast building had been connected by breaking through the walls and installing massive doors.

So now we blindly followed the persons in front of us through the connecting door to the next shelter area and to an emergency exit. Some exits were totally blocked, and people could not get out until the debris was removed.

Finally, we were out in the courtyard. I looked for Papa. Hundreds of people were going in every direction. A few ambulances were screaming their approach, not nearly enough for the desperate need.

I asked people coming out of the various shelters if they had seen my father. Some knew him but had not seen him in the shelter.

Everyone was asked to keep moving on so the emergency workers and volunteers could begin to move the debris and begin their rescue work. I picked my way out to the street.

The main target had been the railroad marshalling yards and tracks. Trains with goods, and the highway underpass through the yard, were all destroyed. Fires were shooting black billows of smoke into the air. The sky over Munich was red.

There were no trains, no streetcars, nothing.

How will I get home? What if the bombers come back? They sometimes come in waves . . . . Well, I can't worry about all the "ifs" now.

I started walking. By train, the trip home was only about 30 minutes.

How long will it take me to walk? Can I find my way home? I have to get home . . . . I have to do it.

Debris everywhere. Some streets were totally blocked by the rubble of destroyed buildings. I had to skirt bomb craters that blocked my way and avoid power lines that lay twisted across the street.

Buildings were burning. Some were roofless ruins. Others looked like giant dollhouses with their façades gone.

Familiar landmarks were unrecognizable or buried under the rubble. Everything looked different. I was no longer sure where I was. All I was aware of was that there were people walking in the same direction I was.

Am I still going the right way, or am I just following other people because it takes less effort . . . because the thought of being alone grips me with panic?

The detours made it seem endless. My eyes burned from the smoke, and my feet hurt, reminding me that my shoes were not only a bit small, but they had hard wooden soles.

I have to sit down and rest . . . not for long . . . just a few minutes . . . .

I sat down on a bench at a deserted streetcar stop. I was glad I had grabbed my sweater when the alarm sounded because now I was feeling chilly. The energy my small lunch had provided had long been used up. Hungry and thirsty, I forced myself to get back up and put one foot in front of the other and keep going. Every now and then, a car or small truck would go by, already filled to capacity with people.

It seemed like I had already walked for hours when a small truck stopped.

"I'm only going as far as Pasing. If that'll help you, there's still room for you in the back," the driver informed me.

"Oh, thank you, thank you, thank you ever so much," I stammered. I was so relieved that I was on the verge of tears. I just knew once I got to Pasing I could make it.

I went to the back of the truck, and two of the people helped pull me up. We were packed like sardines. The ride in the back of the truck was bumpy, but I was grateful not to have to walk for a while. The driver stopped several times to let people off.

In Pasing, I got off and started walking again. At the *Marienplatz*, I walked past the burned-out shells of several streetcars that had never finished their run.

Numbed, I mechanically kept going.

Home . . . away from this nightmare . . . home to Mama, Papa . . . water . . . food . . . and my bed.

The thought of home kept me going. Finally, I was beginning to see the outline of the Dornier Airplane Factory in the distance. I roused from my stupor and panicked.

They've bombed this plant before . . . . Is Mama all right? . . . Is the house still there? Oh, my God, what will I see when I turn the corner? . . .

My heart was pounding as I stopped to get up courage to turn the corner. Even though I was exhausted, I started to run. Turning into our street, I saw the house in the middle of the block. Tears started streaming down my face. Sobbing, I ran. Mama opened the door. Both she and Papa had been frantically watching for me.

I was sobbing and shaking all over. Mama warmed up some soup for me. While I ate, I gradually quieted down. Papa brought me a big shot of Mama's homemade black currant liqueur to drink with my tea while he told me his story.

After the raid he had asked numerous people if they had seen me. All he could find out was that the people in the shelter assigned to the secretarial pool supposedly had gotten out OK through a side

151

exit. Papa then started walking home, but fortunately was able to hitch a ride on a truck that took him most of the way home.

The tea and Mama's liqueur had a calming effect, and soon Mama packed me off to bed. Exhausted physically and mentally, I fell asleep, oblivious to the war and the fact that at any moment the sirens could start their unnerving wail again.

For the next few weeks, the obituary section of the newspaper *Völkischer Beobachter* carried mass announcements listing the dead. No trace was found of several young women from the secretarial pool, who, tired of carrying heavy typewriters, had entered one of the elevators shortly before a bomb hit that elevator shaft.

Later we learned that more than 300 B-17s and B-24s, with fighter escort, had executed the raid.

The heavy bombing had caused such widespread damage that prisoners of war were transported to Munich early every morning to help remove the debris, free trapped people, recover bodies, fill bomb craters, and repair the damaged rail lines.

Because the building where Papa and I worked was damaged so severely, its numerous departments were relocated to wherever space was available in Munich's surrounding area. Papa's office was now in the Arnulfstrasse. Friedl, Martina, and I were assigned to the supplies office in Neuaubing, a twenty-minute walk from my home.

In 1944 alone, Munich suffered more than seventy air raids. Window glass was a commodity that was increasingly difficult to get. People used cardboard, wood, or whatever they had to cover windows blown out by the bombing.

While German cities were being annihilated, Propaganda Minister Goebbels still broadcast his lies about a secret weapon and victory.

*　　*　　*

A SAD AFTERMATH

One morning in February 1945, Martina didn't show up for work. Neither did she show up the next day, or the next. It was the weekend, there had not been any air raids, so I thought she probably had a cold or something. She certainly would return Monday. I could not call her since neither they nor we had a telephone.

On Monday morning, when I arrived at the office, I was told that Martina had died. A pimple on her cheek had become infected and, without the necessary medication, she had died in the hospital. At the cemetery, Friedl and I shed bitter tears as we said good-bye to our friend Martina. We missed Martina's happy spirit terribly.

Chapter 21

To Stay or to Flee?

After my cousin Mariele completed her *Pflichtjahr*, she immediately applied for a job in order to get her ration card. On May 1, 1942, Mariele began working as a secretary for the *Bayrische Staatsministerium für Ernährung and Landwirtschaft*, the Bavarian Ministry of Food and Agriculture, in Munich.

Mariele told us that, in addition to their jobs during the day, two of the employees had to sleep in the office every night in case of an air raid. They were to extinguish incendiary bombs with sand and water provided for that purpose. This task was rotated throughout the office, and everyone was scheduled to take a turn. Weekends were no exception.

A year or two later, neither Mariele nor I remember the exact time, the building where Mariele worked was destroyed during an air raid, and the offices were relocated to Landshut, about forty miles from Munich. Now Mariele was able to come home only on weekends.

In Landshut, Mariele and another employee, Frau Klinger, whose husband was fighting in Russia, were assigned to share a room in a private home. The room was sparsely furnished with two single beds. There was no possibility to cook anything.

Mariele and Frau Klinger ate a cold breakfast at the small table in their assigned room and ate one meal a day in a restaurant. Even though they had to share a small room, they addressed each other formally, as "Mrs. Klinger" and "Miss Riefler" and used the formal "Sie" when speaking to each other as they did in the office.

Mariele eagerly anticipated the weekends she was able to spend at home with her family. Having her own room now seemed like a special privilege to Mariele, and I always looked forward to spending a few hours with her during those weekends. We not only talked about our hopes, dreams and desires but also of our fears, the bombings, and the war. We always treasured our time together, even when Mariele told me of some of the frightening things like the bombing of the train she took to get home every week.

One Friday after work, Mariele was on the train to Munich when the train suddenly stopped in a rural area next to an open field. With the train stopped, she heard the high-pitched howling of air raid sirens in distant towns.

"*Fliegerangriff, alle hinaus,*" air raid, everyone out, was the announcement. There was a mad scramble as everyone hurried to get off the train. People fanned out and threw themselves onto the ground.

"Cover your head with your purse," the soldier lying next to her shouted.

Mariele quickly covered her head with her large leather purse. She felt like an ostrich with its head in the sand, while its body is exposed. Frantically, she tried to press herself into the ground. She was terrified. She had never been out in the open during an air raid.

Fierce firing from the Flak anti-aircraft cannons punctuated the sky, as planes swooped low to strafe the train with machine guns.

While the attack seemed an eternity to Mariele, it actually had lasted only a short time, but it left the train and a large part of the tracks destroyed.

The soldier turned to Mariele, "Are you OK?"

"Yes, I'm all right, and thank you for telling me to use my purse as a cover."

"We lucked out. They wanted the train, not us. The name's Breuer, Martin Breuer," the soldier said as he identified himself.

"Mariele Riefler."

"Well, I guess we should start walking back to Landshut. There won't be a train for a day or so."

Walking along the tracks, they started talking and as they were getting closer to Landshut, Martin offered a suggestion:

"I'm going to get a car from our motor pool and drive to Munich. You're welcome to ride along."

"Thanks, I'd appreciate that. I'm sure my parents will be worried if I don't show up. I take it you live in Munich, too?"

"Nearby, in Obermenzing. I want to get home to my wife and kids."

The walk back to Landshut took a long time. Finally, a few hours later, Mariele and Martin Breuer were again on their way to Munich, this time in a car from the motor pool. Martin offered to pick up Mariele on Fridays on future weekends for the trip to Munich and then again early Monday morning for the trip back to Landshut. Mariele gratefully accepted this offer. Train travel was no longer dependable and often it was necessary to wait for hours in an unheated waiting room.

The Landshut office where Mariele worked was along the banks of the Isar River. As in other German cities, black arrows on the walls of buildings indicated where the nearest air raid shelter was located. Whenever the air raid siren sounded, Mariele and the other employees in her office ran across the bridge to the other side of the river to a large wine cave.

One day, the alarm sounded too late. Planes were already overhead. The street was still full of people headed for the shelter when one of the planes dived down toward the crowd. Everyone was panic-stricken. There was no place to hide.

Miraculously, nothing happened. The plane pulled up again; no shots were fired. Maybe the gunner decided he did not want to shoot at unarmed civilians.

But the scare was enough to convince Mariele and the rest of the office staff to change their pattern. They no longer went to the cave when the alarm sounded but stayed in their offices instead.

With air raids almost a daily occurrence it is no wonder my parents and people in general wondered how much longer the war could possibly go on.

Despite of *Reichspropagandaminister* Goebbels' proclamations to the contrary, we realized that the war, which had been dragging on for more than five long years, was lost. The Allies were on German soil.

While all other bridges across the Rhine River had been blown up on Hitler's orders, U.S. forces had captured the railroad bridge at Remagen. Now the ground fighting was getting closer day by day.

Poking fun at a grave situation that one cannot control is sometimes the only way to accept the inevitable. And so it was with us.

I remember some of the *Galgenhumor,* gallows humor, like the following jokes and song that were circulated by kids quite openly and by older people secretly:

Two friends named Luke and Karl met in Munich. Luke wanted to show Karl his new car. Karl opened the hood to check out the motor.

"But, Luke, your car doesn't even have a motor."

"Oh, that's OK, Karl. I never visit foreign countries, and in Germany it's all going downhill anyway."

And:

"Hey, did you hear that Switzerland has added a Minister of the Navy, and they don't even have a seaport?"

"Well, so what, we also have a Minister of Justice."

We also sang a political version of a popular song:

Es geht alles vorüber, es geht alles vorbei,
Zuerst Adolf Hitler, dann seine Partei.

Everything passes, everything goes away,

First Adolf Hitler, then his party.

To repeat something like this to the wrong person, however, could cost one's life. When did we first realize we actually wanted to be defeated, to be done with this war? Even as we pondered that unspoken question, events were unfolding to bring about the end.

"The Americans will be here by tomorrow." With those words, Mariele's co-worker, Frau Klinger, stormed into the office. She was visibly out of breath.

"And we don't want to be caught with these damn things. Help me, Miss Riefler," continued Frau Klinger, who never swore.

With that, she climbed on a chair and took the mandatory Hitler picture off the wall. Mariele took down the swastika flag. They ran across the street and threw both items into the Isar River.

Returning, they almost collided with Martin Breuer. Entering the office with them, Martin addressed Mariele: "I took a car from the motor pool. I am now AWOL. When the Americans get to Munich, I want to be with my family. Do you want a ride home?"

Frau Klinger protested, "But Fräulein Riefler, Munich is a large city, and the fighting there will be heavy. You'll be safer here with us."

"Yes, Landshut is a small town and a hospital town at that," another one of her colleagues added. "There'll be little, if any, fighting here."

"You could be stuck here for some time, if you don't leave now," warned Martin Breuer.

"I want to get home and be with my family, no matter what," Mariele said. She turned to Martin and asked, "Do we have time to stop by my room, so I can grab my suitcase?"

After stopping to get her things, Martin and Mariele headed for Munich in the *Holzbrenner,* one of the World War II wood-burning cars that Martin had "requisitioned" from the motor pool. Since these cars created quite a bit of smoke, the two were in constant danger of being detected by an SS unit.

In order to avoid detection, they drove on the less traveled country roads. When they finally arrived at Mariele's house, her parents were overjoyed. They offered Martin some coffee, but he declined.

"Thanks, but I'm really anxious to get home and prepare for whatever is to come. You take care tomorrow."

As it turned out, Landshut would not have offered Mariele the relative safety that her co-workers suggested. The fighting for Landshut between the German 38th SS Grenadier Division and two American armored tank forces pressing the 38th on both flanks was unexpectedly heavy. The next day, April 29, 1945, the German 38th moved through Landshut, across the River Isar, hoping to set up a defense line south of the city. Unable to accomplish this, the Germans were forced to retreat, leaving the way for the American troops to move on to their next destination.

Mariele's flight from Landshut to her home in Munich was the signal for us that the wished-for end of the war was imminent. We knew that the Allied troops were bearing down upon us, but, one way or the other, the nightmare we were living would soon be over. Munich's fate would be decided within a couple of days.

Chapter 22

The Occupation

The surrender of Munich on April 30, 1945, had been a relief to both the conquered and the conqueror. Major bloodshed had been avoided and a welcome quiet now lay over the city.

The day after the surrender of Munich, a strict curfew was announced by the U.S. Occupation Forces. It allowed us to be outside for a few hours in the early afternoon. We fed the chickens and rabbits and brought in the first tender lettuces and radishes from the hot frame in our garden.

The U.S. Occupation Headquarters for our area was set up in the elementary school that I had attended. We also were informed of the time when all guns, rifles, pistols, and ammunition had to be surrendered at headquarters.

The war was over, but our lives were lived on a precarious roller coaster, alternating between hope and resignation. We didn't know what to expect from those who were now in charge. Would they treat us well, or would they victimize us? It was difficult to interpret their behavior, and the language barrier didn't help.

One of the waitresses from the brewery and restaurant at the corner of *Landsbergerstrasse* came to get Mariele. The woman was visibly upset and worried. She told my aunt that a U.S. officer and several soldiers were at the restaurant. The officer was extremely angry. No one at the restaurant could understand him. They were afraid and asked Mariele to come and translate.

When Mariele entered the room, the officer yelled at her:

"Do you know how we like the Germans? . . . I'll tell you. Six feet under."

Mariele was terrified.

"I am here to translate. These people don't speak English," she said.

The officer was momentarily stunned, then continued in a much more civil tone and asked Mariele where she had acquired her proficiency in English.

Mariele translated the officer's requests for lodging and cooking facilities for his men without any more hostility. She was relieved when she was finished interpreting and was allowed to leave. She was deeply disturbed.

"He must have had a terrible experience to have that much anger; maybe he lost a friend or relative in the war," Mariele's mother told her after hearing Mariele's story.

We found a possible answer to his hateful outburst some time later, when the first newspapers were printed again and we stared at photos of the Dachau concentration camp with its piles of emaciated bodies.

And then we read the names of more and more concentration and underground work camps in vast areas of Germany.

Was this American propaganda? We had surmised that what went on in the concentration camps was bad, but if these pictures were the truth, how could we live with this knowledge? We could not believe that these atrocities actually had been committed in the name of the German people.

While we no longer had to worry about air raids, life was far from normal, and there was still plenty of uncertainty and worry in our daily lives. Like us, families all over were eager to hear the fate of their soldiers. The last we had heard from Ludwig was in January 1945. Was he alive? Was he a prisoner of war? We knew, to be a prisoner in Russia, was to be in constant danger.

Gradually, German soldiers returned one by one to their families, or a family received word that their loved one would never come back.

And so it was after the first month of Occupation that Mama and I went to the Evangelical Church to attend the memorial service for my friend and first secret love, Herbert. His parents had not heard from him during the last few months until they got the heartbreaking news of his death.

From the fall of 1944 to the end of the war, as Germany needed more and more soldiers to replenish the army, twelve to sixteen year olds were drafted. When these boy soldiers, who had not received adequate training, panicked and fled in the face of overwhelming enemy numbers and equipment, they were often shot in the back by the SS. My friend Herbert was one of them. They found his body along with several others in a shallow trench, shot in the back of the neck.

During Herbert's memorial my thoughts strayed . . . . *It seemed so long ago when we both took the train to Pasing to attend school, and we walked together to the train station. It was a case of puppy love. We had schemed to go to the movies together, and I had dreamed of maybe holding hands in the darkness of the movie theater, maybe even receiving my first kiss. But it was not to be. We were too young, our parents had said, so we never got to share that first innocent kiss. Ironically, Herbert was not too young to die for Hitler.*

The end of the service interrupted my thoughts. People were starting to leave. Mama and I stopped to talk to Herbert's family. His mother turned to me and said:

"I knew you'd be here. Herbert would have wanted you to have this," she said as she reached into her purse and gave me a photo of Herbert. I think maybe she knew about our youthful infatuation.

During the early days of the occupation, we quickly came to realize that our greatest immediate threat was not the Occupation Forces themselves but the Russian forced laborers whom the Occupation Forces had freed. The laborers were the individuals who had been marched by our house daily on their way to and from work at the nearby Dornier Aircraft Factory.

This is my friend Herbert. We were considered too young
to go to the movies together, but he was not too young
to die for Hitler.

German citizens were not allowed to be out of the house at night;
they would be shot on sight. But the freed Russians had no curfew.
They were able to come and go as they pleased, and they were angry.
They had been brought to Germany against their will, and some
of them started to terrorize our neighborhood and to roam the
countryside.

Worse still, some had somehow obtained weapons and could force
themselves into our houses and do what they wanted. So we lived
with the added menace of the roaming and marauding Russians.

One day, the bell on our garden gate rang. Three Russians were
standing at the gate.

"Hurry up and hide in the attic," Papa told me. Then he slowly
went to unlock the gate. The Russians walked up the drive and into
the house.

"You give man clothes, we no hurt you," one of the Russians,
pistol in hand, explained in broken German.

The Russians began to look around. They took our big radio in the living room, the one that could bring in broadcasts from foreign countries. Papa quickly collected some of his and Ludwig's clothes and handed them over. They indicated they wanted him to go outside with them.

"You have car in there?" they asked, pointing to the locked garage.

"No, no car . . . . We have no car."

"You open door," they demanded. Papa got the key and unlocked the garage. Finding no car, they took our two bicycles and left.

"We'll miss the radio and the bikes, but we are lucky no one was hurt. Just maybe they remembered the fruit we gave them," Mama voiced her relief.

"We can always borrow a bike from Marie and Willie when we need one. And as for the radio, we still have the little radio in the kitchen." Papa added.

We were not the only ones in our family to have a frightening encounter with Russians. Uncle Willie and Mariele also found themselves victimized by them.

Now that the worst was over, Uncle Willie wanted to check on the Breuer family and thank Herr Breuer for getting Mariele back safely the day before the surrender of Munich, so Uncle Willie and Mariele got on their bikes and started out for the small town of Obermenzing, where the Breuer family lived.

Not quite halfway to their destination, two Russians barred the road and demanded their bicycles. Uncle Willie and Mariele handed over the bikes and started the long walk home. Now both of our families were without bikes. Our only mode of transportation was gone.

It was almost a year later before Mariele and Uncle Willie were finally able to thank Martin Breuer.

The most serious incident involving the Russians happened late one night about midnight when my parents and I were awakened by blood-curdling screams. Running to the window and looking out from behind the curtains, we could see several Russians forcing a woman at gunpoint down the street toward their camp. No one could help her. She was found dead outside the gate of the Russian compound the next morning. Her screams haunted me for a long time.

The next day, during the time the curfew was lifted, Aunt Marie, Uncle Willie, and Mariele stopped by our house and told us they were going to the local U.S. Occupation Headquarters.

They planned to tell the officer in charge that the deeds committed by the Russians were as bad as the bombings. Even though I was a little afraid of what could happen, I pleaded until they allowed me to come along.

Two soldiers were on guard duty at the entrance of the school. This time, I looked at their faces. They didn't look fierce or mean. They looked relaxed as they were leaning on their guns and chewing on something. I had never seen soldiers on duty this relaxed.

My uncle told them we would like to see the officer in charge. The soldier was obviously surprised but pleased to hear English and asked him and also Mariele several questions. Soon they were talking about life in the States. The other soldier on guard duty also started talking to Mariele and her parents. Finally, the first soldier left to go and report to his officer.

When he came back, he asked us to follow him.

In the former principal's office, we met the commander. Mariele and her parents introduced themselves and me and explained that they had lived in Westchester County, New York, until the spring of 1938. They had brought along papers to prove what they were saying. Aunt Marie and Uncle Willie proceeded to explain what had happened the night before and explained the robberies at gunpoint in our part of town.

The officer indicated he had received the report of the gang rape and murder of the night before. He asked a lot more questions and jotted down my uncle's name and address. The officer left, and when he came back, he informed my aunt and uncle that he would set up a telephone center in their house.

Shifts of three soldiers were to man the post twenty-four hours a day until further notice. My aunt and uncle thanked the officer and headed for home. Mariele said she was going on to the Signal Corps that was located in the former Dornier Aircraft Factory.

"I've written a letter to Aunt Katherine letting her know that we survived, and telling her about Ludwig. I am sure she and our relatives in the States are terribly worried about us."

"How are you planning to mail it?" Uncle Willie asked in surprise.

"I am going to wait at the gate and talk to the first friendly looking GI. I'll tell him about my grandmother and aunt worrying about us. I left the envelope open, so he can check the contents."

"I don't know, I guess it's worth a try," answered Uncle Willie. "But I'll go with you."

"Can I come too, please? I really, really want to," I pleaded.

Soon the three of us were on the way to the former Dornier Werk, now the base of the Signal Corps.

"Why are all of the soldiers chewing tobacco, like old men do?" I asked Mariele.

"That's gum they're chewing," she informed me.

"Gum?" I asked perplexed. I had never heard of chewing gum.

Again the guards seemed totally relaxed as they chewed their gum and leaned on their rifles. I secretly started to call them "chewing gum soldiers."

We didn't have to wait long until two GIs came through the gate. And that is how Mariele met Frank. He was the first GI to come through the gate with his buddy, Ralph.

"Hi, do you have a minute?" she asked. "My name's Mary, this is my father, Willie Riefler, and this is my cousin Anneliese. My parents and I lived in New York before the war. My grandmother and aunt still live there, and I know they're terribly worried about us, and I wondered . . ."

The two young GIs were immediately interested in this German girl and her father who both spoke with a New York accent and asked them some more questions. Finally, the one named Frank took the letter and said he would read it and mail it. He also asked where they lived in case there was a reply. On our way home, Mariele voiced her concern.

"I hope he actually mails the letter and doesn't just toss it. He did seem sincere, I thought."

"Well, at least we tried to get news to *Grossmama* and Aunt Katherine," I tried to assure her, and after a short good-bye I hurried home because of the curfew.

Mariele and her father had been home only a couple of hours when the first three soldiers, who were to man the telephone center, arrived at their house. They parked their Jeep in front of the house and proceeded to set up their equipment in the living room.

There was nothing for the soldiers to do except sit by the phone and be alert to what was going on in the area. They brought magazines and books to occupy their time, and when they had read them, they left them for Mariele and her parents.

I was the next one in line, and I always felt I had inherited a treasure. My dictionary got a real work-out as I tried to read the stories. My vocabulary increased because I wrote each new word in a notebook and practiced the new words until they became part of my active vocabulary. Even though there was a no-fraternization order, the soldiers enjoyed talking English with Mariele and her parents. They even encouraged me in my attempts at English.

The constant presence of the Army Jeep alone did much to stop the aggression and looting in our area. People in the neighborhood were relieved to see the Jeep in front of Mariele's house. It was a beacon of safety for them.

The radio station for the U.S. Forces was American Forces Network, AFN Munich. One of the programs was called "Bouncing in Bavaria." It played all of the popular American songs. We still had the small radio, and when it was time for "Bouncing in Bavaria," I was poised with pad and pencil to write down as many of the song lyrics as I could.

Later I asked Mariele to fill in the missing words. This is how I first became acquainted with the songs of Frank Sinatra, Bing Crosby, and the many other singing stars of the 1940s.

I also listened to the American news. Mama and Papa weren't always too happy when I took over the radio. Papa was especially upset because listening to the news and the weather report was a daily ritual for him.

When it was time for the news, I had to quickly switch the radio to the *Süddeutscher Rundfunk,* South German Radio, for him.

Whenever possible, I went to Mariele's house to practice my English on the soldiers. I also made my personal acquaintance with chewing gum. One of the soldiers gave me some gum, and I chewed it for a while as I had seen them do.

After a while the flavor was gone, and my jaws were tired of chewing, so I swallowed it. When Mariele realized this, she told me that I should have taken the gum out and thrown it away. I couldn't understand why. It seemed such a waste to just throw it away.

After the Russian forced workers were returned to Russia, the telephone post in my aunt and uncle's house ended. Mariele and I were sad to see the soldiers leave. We had enjoyed our conversations. Getting the American books and magazines to read had been an added bonus.

I was at Mariele's house one Sunday several weeks later, when the doorbell rang. It was Frank and Ralph, the soldiers from the Signal Corps. Frank had a letter and a package from Aunt Katherine. She had sent Frank some home-baked cookies as a little thank you for mailing Mariele's letter.

All of our relatives in the United States were so relieved to know we had survived the war. Aunt Katherine also had included a letter for us and in the package with Frank's cookies was coffee, tins of meat, and a can of Crisco for Mariele's and my family to share.

Overjoyed, Mariele's mother made some coffee right away. Frank shared his cookies. It was a wonderful afternoon coffee, reminding us of the pleasure of afternoon coffee before the war.

In her letter, Aunt Katherine asked if she could send Frank more food packages for us. She wrote that he should always open the package and check its content. As much as she wanted to help us, she did not want him to get into any trouble.

"It's OK with me. Who knows, maybe she'll bake some more cookies for me," Frank joked.

The war was over, but the hunger was not. The official ration was about 1,100 calories a day, but food was not always available.

Again we were lucky. We had the garden, the chickens, and the rabbits. Mama always shared some vegetables, fruit, a few eggs, and part of a chicken or rabbit with Aunt Therese whose husband, my Uncle Georg, had a weak heart and passed away in 1944 during one of the air raids. Living alone in the city, my aunt had no way to supplement her ration cards by making a garden or by keeping chickens or rabbits.

When the next package from Aunt Katherine arrived, Frank opened it with us. It was like manna from heaven. There was a big tin of bacon grease, enough to cook with for several months. Aunt Katherine and some of her friends had strained and rendered their bacon grease, filled a gallon olive oil tin with it, and Uncle Joe had sealed it shut. We were all starved for any kind of fat. Potatoes from our garden and eggs fried in bacon grease were like a gourmet meal to us.

There were also clothing articles for Mariele and me. Some of Aunt Katherine's friends had given her clothing their daughters no longer wore. We could not imagine someone giving away nice clothing like this and eagerly tried on everything. We had our own little style show. Everything Aunt Katherine sent was always split between our two families.

To the consternation of my mother, Aunt Katherine had included some red nail polish for Mariele and me. During the war, there had been big posters that portrayed Eleanor Roosevelt, the wife of the American president, with bright red lipstick and red fingernail polish, while it showed a German woman in work clothes working for the war effort in a factory.

Red fingernail polish, lipstick, and makeup had been portrayed as American decadence during the war. I liked red fingernails in spite of the poster and in spite of their decadence. The movie stars I had seen in Mariele's scrapbooks wore makeup and red fingernail polish, and I wanted fingernails like theirs.

Mama thought that wearing red fingernail polish was just not decent, that it made a girl look provocative. Mariele's mother thought it was OK. She was used to the young girls in the United States wearing nail polish.

I just could not give up the nail polish, so Mama made me wear gloves anytime I went someplace with her. I wore gloves a lot that year.

It was always a special day when a package from Aunt Katherine arrived. But one day Mariele came to our house quite excited and told me that Aunt Katherine had sent us some popcorn. I had never heard of popcorn and, when she showed it to me, all I could think of was chicken feed.

"We need some oil to pop this," Mariele said, and proceeded to get out a pan.

"I'm not wasting our good oil on this chicken feed. Throw it to the chickens, and they'll lay some eggs."

"You don't understand . . . . OK, I'll bring you some of our oil if you let me fix it."

She convinced me, so I begrudgingly gave her some oil. When all at once it sounded like bullets popped around in that pan, I got scared and told her to get rid of it quickly before someone got hurt. That was my introduction to popcorn.

Frank and Ralph started to stop by, even if there was no package or letter from Aunt Katherine. We listened to Mariele's American records, and sometimes we sang along. One evening we were listening to the records again. My feet were keeping time with the music.

"May I have this dance, Twinkle Toes?" Ralph said, laughing.

Reaching for my hand, he led me out into the long hallway where we could dance. I loved it.

Frank and Mariele joined us and soon we were dancing to "Red Sails in the Sunset," the "Peanut Vendor," "Harbor Lights," "Stardust," and many of the old American records Mariele had brought with her before the war.

To Frank and Ralph, the songs meant home. For Mariele, the songs were a reminder of her life in America, where she had been happy before the war.

I loved to dance with Ralph. It was a new experience for me to dance with a young man. The last time I had danced with a boy was when I was twelve years old in dancing class. That seemed so far in the past . . . .

My friend Johanna and I had been so excited when our parents enrolled us in a course at a dance studio across from the Munich Opera. Once a week, we took the train to Munich and then walked to the studio. I remembered how embarrassed we were at first. Later, we started to enjoy the lessons. One of the boys developed a crush on me, and he and his friend escorted Johanna and me to the railroad station after class. After 1940, dancing in public was prohibited, and when the air raids began, our lessons ended. The new friendships had ended before they really had a chance to get started. As the war progressed, it seems my friends and I became much older than our years, and we lost the ability to laugh and giggle over nothing like teenage girls are prone to do.

Now, after all the years of war, blackouts, fear and bombs, I enjoyed dancing and singing the American songs I had learned. Ralph and I became good friends. He told me about his high school sweetheart back in the States and showed me her picture. They had become engaged before he had shipped out for overseas. I thought she was very pretty. Ralph was to be shipped home soon, and he was counting the days.

My dancing was not without a price. Afterwards, when I was alone, I felt guilty for dancing and laughing when I didn't know where Ludwig was. I could not bear to think that my brother might not be alive. I knew Ludwig had to come back to us.

There were many things besides English words I did not know. I did not know what a grapefruit was. Ralph arrived one day with a can of grapefruit juice for us to try. He said to drink it in the morning with breakfast. The next morning I poured a glass for my parents and me, and after taking a sip, I quickly spit it out again.

When Ralph asked a few days later how we had liked the juice, I told him that unfortunately it was spoiled. While I never became a fan of popcorn or chewing gum, I did learn to enjoy grapefruit.

Gradually, some basic order began to emerge, and both Mariele and I had returned to our former jobs. The railroad had miles and miles of track to reconstruct, railroad stations to rebuild, and trains to get running again. It was a daunting and frustrating job, considering the scarcity of manpower and materials.

Mariele, at the Bavarian Ministry for Food and Agriculture, translated in meetings with the Food and Agriculture Branch of the military government. The war also had taken its toll on livestock. The retreating soldiers had butchered animals to feed themselves. Farmers had slaughtered animals in the war's last few weeks of disorganization and disorder when no one was keeping track anymore.

Now the job was to ascertain how much livestock was available for breeding, for milk production, and for consumption. Stringent rationing was still in effect, and the Occupation Forces had to establish guidelines on how to proceed.

The air raids were over, but Germany's cities were destroyed. Families were living in basement ruins or were scattered or displaced. Posted on the ruins of some of the destroyed buildings were messages for relatives: *Mona R. and daughter are living with Cousin Magda K. on Wittelsbacher Street.*

Restoring homes and families couldn't take place until the tons of rubble were cleared away, and the rebuilding could begin.

Three million German men had been killed in the war. Others were still held as prisoners of war or were disabled. Therefore, the gargantuan task of cleaning up the debris and the recovery of bodies still buried under the rubble was left to the *Trümmerfrauen,* the rubble women, of the cities.

Makeshift crosses on top of destroyed buildings indicated bodies were still buried underneath. As the first summer after the war wore on, the larger German cities began to smell from the cadavers still under the rubble.

In colored headscarves and gloves, the rubble women of Munich used hammers to painstakingly clean the mortar off usable bricks. The bricks were stacked and the remaining rubble was loaded into carts which, in lieu of horses or mules, the women often had to pull away themselves.

These women recovered the corpses buried in the rubble and worked untiringly to reclaim their city, building by building, block by block.

Every unemployed woman between ages sixteen and forty-five was required to help in this process, unless she was a student, had small children, or was sick or disabled. To be able to perform this hard labor, they received extra ration coupons.

In many German cities, one can today find memorials to these "rubble women" who actually started the long drawn-out healing process for the destroyed cities.

With so many buildings destroyed, those that were intact were choice picks for the Occupation Forces when they began to requisition private homes for their officers. Our house was among the ones selected.

We were given one day's notice to vacate our house. We were to take only clothing and other necessary items. All furniture and dishes were to be left. We were devastated by this order. Where were we to go? Aunt Marie and Uncle Willie already had their nephew, his wife, and their two little boys living with them. Their house had been destroyed three years ago during an air raid on the Eifel region of Germany. With millions of refugees from the eastern part of Germany and the bombed cities who had fled and sought refuge in Bavaria, there was not a room to spare.

The evacuation order had been issued by Frank's commanding officer. Frank went to his superior and told him that he knew the people living in the house he had requisitioned.

Frank told him that the woman's mother, sister, and family lived in New York and had lived there since after World War I. He added that the man of the house was a disabled veteran of World War I who had become a member of the NSDAP (the Nazi Party) only in order to keep his job with the railroad and never had been active in the party nor attended party meetings.

Frank also added that, with their son still missing in Russia, this family had a lot to deal with. Aside from this, three rooms of the house had been assigned to refugees from Hamburg and an employee for the railroad.

The officer decided he wanted to meet us himself. He ordered Frank to accompany him to our house that evening. Mariele was to interpret.

The officer and Frank arrived. Mariele had come earlier. Mama was a bundle of nerves. Her constant worry about Ludwig and now this. It was simply too much for her. She had burst out in tears several times during the afternoon.

The officer started to direct his questions to Papa. He wanted to know where Papa had served in World War I and how he became disabled. Papa told him and showed him how he could manipulate the prosthesis he had. This went on for quite a while.

Then the officer directed some questions to Mama and me. He asked about Mama's mother and sister in the States. Finally, he asked me where I worked.

The officer also seemed quite interested in the books in the large bookcase and, pointing to the row of Karl May books, he said:

"Long ago, I read some of these. Are they yours?"

"They're my brother's, but I've read every one of them."

"Sergeant Romano tells me your brother is missing in Russia. Is that right?"

"Yes, it is. The last we heard from him was last January."

Without another word, the officer turned to Frank and informed him that he was ready to leave.

We didn't know how to interpret this rather abrupt departure. It certainly did not give us any idea whether or not to be hopeful. We were in turmoil. Should we start packing and take some things to my aunt and uncle's house?

"There is only about half an hour before the curfew starts," I reminded my parents.

"First of all, we'll make a list of what we need to pack, then we'll pack. In the morning, as soon as the curfew is off, we'll take things to Willie and Marie's to store in their attic or wherever we can," Papa decided.

Making the list meant making lots of difficult choices. We were all so nervous and upset it took every bit of our willpower to concentrate on this job.

Mariele had gone home to wait and see if Frank would come back. It was almost midnight when the doorbell at Mariele's house rang, and Frank told her he had good news: We would not have to move. They both hurried the few houses down the street to tell us. Since Mariele was accompanied by a U.S. serviceman, it was safe for her to be out after curfew.

To say that we were most thankful would be an understatement. The day had been physically and mentally exhausting and unnerving. It seems once our anxiety was relieved, all energy drained from our bodies. Mama brewed some peppermint tea to soothe and calm us and gave a huge sigh as she voiced her opinion: "Tomorrow has to be better."

We sipped our tea, and finally, after one o'clock in the morning, we made our way to bed.

When I said my usual prayers and my special prayers for Ludwig that night, I also gave thanks for being able to be in my own bed, something for which I had never thanked God before.

Chapter 23

Our Friend Ingrid

I am stepping out of my memoir for a short time to devote this chapter to Ingrid, Mariele's best friend, because her life had been closely entwined with Mariele's and mine. It is the trajectory of a young girl's life in Germany before, during, and after the war.

Ingrid's story shows another way lives were changed drastically by the circumstances of war. While Mariele and I were anticipating our departure for America, Ingrid's life had taken a different turn.

It was 1939 when Ingrid and my cousin Mariele met. Ingrid was a year older than Mariele and lived with her mother and stepfather just a block from Mariele's house. Ingrid's mother was a kind and warm person, but her stepfather was very strict and did not allow her to have many friends.

Luckily, he approved of Mariele and her parents, so Ingrid was allowed to be friends with Mariele. In the evenings, Ingrid often came to Mariele's house where they talked, crocheted, and knitted while listening to records of songs Mariele had brought with her from America. Ingrid was learning English in school, so she was always eager to speak English with Mariele.

Sometimes they were allowed to go to the movies together and that was always a special treat for them.

"Do you think you can go to the new movie at the Ufa Palast?" Mariele asked Ingrid.

"I'll ask. You know it's restricted. Think we can get in?"

"We're both tall so I think we can pass," Mariele assured Ingrid.

Certain movies in Germany were restricted. Some were for viewers 14 years or older, for others, one had to be at least 18 years. Members of the local police force came into the theater after people were seated, or after the *Wochenschau,* the wartime newsreels, to check the audience.

The cheapest tickets were the third-place tickets, the first few rows closest to the screen. The younger crowd tended to buy those tickets. These rows were always scrutinized thoroughly by the police. Anyone who did not look old enough was asked for an ID. If the police found someone who was under the age limit, he or she was kicked out, which was embarrassing and costly because they lost the money they had paid for the ticket.

For this reason, we spent a little more to buy second-place tickets when we tried to "pass." The scrutiny was not quite as thorough there. We never bought first-class, or *Sperrsitz,* the seats in the back, which were much more expensive.

I often envied Mariele and Ingrid when they were able to see a movie that I couldn't because I was too young. I never failed to cajole Mariele long enough until she told me "all about it." I sometimes felt jealous of the time Mariele spent with Ingrid. That was to change soon as I began to see more of Mariele and Ingrid once I was enrolled in the Hitler Youth.

In 1939, membership in the Hitler Youth became compulsory for boys and girls. All other youth organizations were banned. The girls movement of the Hitler Youth was the *Bund Deutscher Mädchen,* or *BDM,* League of German Girls, for girls ages fourteen to eighteen. Girls ten to fourteen were in the *Jungmädel,* Young Girls League.

One day, during my last class in school, the girls in my class were signed up to become members of the *Jungmädel,* while the boys became members of the *Hitlerjugend.*

On the *Führer's* birthday, in a hall with flags and much fanfare, we, the new inductees, became children of the Reich and the *Führer.* From now on, our life belonged to Hitler. I actually don't remember much of the actual ceremony, the speakers, or the speeches.

This is me at age 10 in my *Jungmädel*
(Young Girls League) uniform.

Ingrid, and a year later Mariele, were appointed to become group leaders, *Scharführerinnen*, of the younger group, of which I was a member. The idea was for "youth to be led by youth," not by adults. All *Jungmädel* had to wear a special uniform—a navy blue skirt, a white blouse with a black neckerchief—to meetings. The neckerchief was secured with a woven leather slide, the *Knoten*.

We met twice a week, on Wednesdays after school, and on Saturdays. Previously we had school on Saturdays until noon. Now Saturday classes were cancelled, and we attended our *Jungmädel* meetings instead.

I felt that was quite OK, though my parents would rather have had me in school. In fact, my parents were not thrilled about some of the meetings, but parents did not have much to say where the Hitler Youth was concerned. Attendance was obligatory.

Our Saturday *Jungmädel* meeting was usually set aside for gymnastics and other sports. We went to the *Turnhalle* where we exercised on the rings and the horse and did rhythmic gymnastics with Indian clubs. Sometimes we practiced spear throwing in the empty meadow across from Ingrid's house.

We also marched and sang the new songs we had practiced: *"Oh, du schöner Westerwald,"* about the beautiful forest by that name, or *"Die blauen Dragoner sie reiten,"* about the blue cavalry riding with their flags blowing in the wind and others. The *Westerwald* song was my favorite. We also had to practice some political songs, like the Horst Wessel song about the SA marching.

On our Wednesday after-school meetings, we learned songs, worked on crafts, and filled out pages of the required *Ahnenpass*, ancestry research. A printed booklet had been provided for this purpose.

Everyone had to record their ancestors as far back as could be documented, at least to 1800. We did not question why we were researching our ancestors. It was just something we did. At the age of ten, I had no idea of the hidden, sinister purpose of my *Ahnenpass*. When the booklet was finished, it had to be verified and stamped by the local *Standesamt,* Bureau of Vital Statistics.

On special weekends, we went on daytrips to attractions nearby. A few times during the summer we camped out, cooked our own evening meal, and then sang songs around a roaring campfire. While I was not a fan of the marching, I did like the camping out and singing around the campfire.

In wintertime, the *Jungmädel,* as well as the older *BDM* groups, sold pins and medallions for the *Winterhilfe,* winter help, in the streets. People wore the pins on coat lapels to show that they had "given to the cause." The money derived from the *Winterhilfe* was to provide warm clothing and heating materials for poor families during the winter. It was always a competition to see who could sell the most.

After the war started, our *Jungmädel* meetings included instruction in first aid. We also knit wrist and ear warmers, mittens, scarves, and socks which were desperately needed by the soldiers who often lacked the warm things necessary to withstand the frigid Russian winter.

When Mariele started her duty year and Ingrid took a job, new leaders were appointed for our group. But after 1942, with the air raids increasing, meetings became erratic. Meeting places often were destroyed or had to be used for other purposes.

After Ingrid finished her schooling, she worked at the *Finanzamt*, Internal Finance Office, in Munich. If I remember correctly, it was in 1944, the week after Ingrid's twentieth birthday that part of the *Finanzamt* was severely damaged during a massive air raid on Munich. English prisoners of war were brought in every morning to help clear away the rubble and recover any bodies still under the debris.

One day, a German guard in charge of the prisoners came into the office where Ingrid worked and asked if anyone spoke English. He needed someone to translate. Ingrid's boss volunteered Ingrid to do the translating.

That is how Ingrid met Harry, one of the English prisoners of war. From that day on, Ingrid was called upon to translate between the guards and the prisoners of war.

It wasn't long before Ingrid and Harry also started to have private conversations. Harry told her he was from the London area. His plane had been shot down over Munich. Later, they looked for ways to see each other more and started to meet in one of the bomb-damaged rooms that was still furnished but was no longer used as office space.

When Ingrid told Mariele of her clandestine meetings with Harry, Mariele tried to warn Ingrid. She reminded Ingrid about the terrible consequences for both Ingrid and Harry should their meetings be discovered.

One morning, after a long air raid during the night, Ingrid felt ill and could not go to the office. She asked Mariele to give Harry a note from her.

When Mariele arrived at the place where the prisoners worked, there was no guard close by, so she was able to speak to Harry. He indicated for Mariele to follow him. They were in one of the bomb-damaged rooms, conversing quietly, when they heard heavy boots approaching.

"Get in there, quickly," Harry whispered and pushed Mariele into a small closed hall area.

Then Harry started to clear rubble from the damaged area on the other side of the room.

The guard came into the room, nodded to Harry and walked on.

When she was sure the guard was gone, Mariele came out of hiding. She was shaking all over.

"What would you have done if he would have stopped to investigate?" Mariele questioned Harry.

"I would have had no choice but to kill him" was Harry's answer.

Mariele managed to pull herself together and hurried back out to the street where she got sick and vomited.

The whole episode had been so totally terrifying that Mariele told Ingrid never to ask her to carry messages to Harry again.

About half a year later, Ingrid told Mariele that she was pregnant with Harry's child.

"I haven't told my mom yet. I know she will be devastated at first, but she will help me. The thought of telling my stepfather scares me to death," Ingrid confided to Mariele.

"I don't know what to tell you. But, remember, you can come to us anytime you need to get away" was all Mariele said to comfort her. It was frightening news.

Ingrid wanted to tell her mother. She hated having to lie to her mother, but she could not tell her that the baby was from an English prisoner of war. Her story was that the baby was from a soldier she had met at work, who was now on the Russian front. Her mother was deeply upset. Finally, they decided to put off telling her stepfather for as long as possible.

As an expectant mother, Ingrid applied for an extra ration card. She continued to work and as far as everyone knew she was expecting the baby of a soldier who was on the Russian front. Mariele was the only person who knew that it was Harry's child, the child of a prisoner of war. The truth would have had tragic repercussions.

Ingrid's stepfather was a very angry man when Ingrid and her mom told him that Ingrid was pregnant. He told her that she was a fallen woman. Women who had a baby out of wedlock were looked down upon in those days. Some mothers warned their daughters of what happens when girls "gave themselves" to a man before they were married.

The months went on, and the war finally ended. The Allied forces freed the prisoners of war. Harry came to look for Ingrid. He knew that she was pregnant, and he wanted to tell her good-bye before he was returned to England.

Ingrid's parents' house had a balcony along the back of the house, and Ingrid saw Harry from there. He was heading toward her house. She left the house, and he followed her to a bombed-out building where they could talk.

Harry avowed his love for her and the baby, told her good-bye, and said he would write to her. He also promised to apply to get permission for her and the baby to join him in England as soon as possible.

Ingrid faithfully wrote to Harry but weeks went by and then months, and she didn't hear from him. Her consolation was to go to Mariele's house. Here she could talk openly with Mariele about Harry and the baby she carried.

When it was time for Ingrid to have her baby, Mariele's friends, Frank and Bob, soldiers of the U.S. Signal Corps, got a covered truck from the motor pool, put a lounge chair in the truck bed, then picked up Ingrid and Mariele and proceeded to the hospital. Mariele and Ingrid were hidden in the back of the truck, as the no fraternization law was still in effect.

Mariele stayed with Ingrid until the baby was born. It was a healthy boy.

As soon as she could, Ingrid wrote to Harry and told him that their son was born. She was sure that she would now hear from him. No letter came from him, and the letters she sent never came back.

Ingrid's joy was her little boy, whom she had named Robert. We saw her go by with little Bobby in the baby carriage many times. She was completely devoted to the little one. Ingrid was nursing him, and the baby was doing well.

It was the summer of 1946. Soon Bobby would be one year old, and Ingrid decided she would stop nursing him then. She also made another decision. She had been sending letters and photos of Bobby to Harry.

Ingrid, with little Bobby.

She now wrote Harry another letter with the latest picture of Bobby. In the letter, she told Harry that, unless she heard from him, this would be the last letter he would receive from her.

Ingrid waited for a response to her last letter, which never came. To help herself cope, she maintained her usual routine. Every day after Ingrid came home from work, she put Bobby in the baby carriage and they went for a walk. One particular day, Ingrid, with Bobby in the carriage, stopped at Mariele's house. Ingrid couldn't wait to tell Mariele that Bobby had said "Mama" for the first time. She was bursting with the joyful news.

Later that same night, the baby became sick. Ingrid rushed him to the hospital, where it was determined he had a constricted bowel. By morning, Bobby was dead.

Ingrid's first big love had left her with a broken heart. Now her baby, the focal point of her life, was gone. Ingrid was devastated. She deeply mourned for Bobby, and several times a week we would see her walk past our house to the cemetery. In her hands, she always had a little bouquet of flowers for Bobby.

Although she could have sold the milk that she continued to pump from her breasts, Ingrid's heart went out to two young mothers who did not have enough milk for their babies, so she gave her milk to them, thereby helping them to keep their babies strong and healthy.

About a year after Bobby's death, Mariele and I came to the United States. Mariele kept in close contact with Ingrid, who still worked at the *Finanzamt* in Munich. She was a conscientious and skilled employee and was well-liked by her colleagues.

Several years passed. Munich, like other cities in Germany, was busy reconstructing and getting back to a normal semblance of existence. The annual party for the employees of the *Finanzamt* was coming up.

"Are you coming to the yearly office party this Saturday afternoon?" Ingrid's friend Rita asked.

"Thanks for asking me, but I don't think so."

"Else and I are both going, and we'd really like you to join us. We'll have a nice time together," Rita pleaded.

"There will be good food, and you really need to get out. We won't take no for an answer," Else joined in.

"Well, I guess I've been outvoted." Ingrid smiled and agreed to meet them.

The party was in full swing, and a band was playing when Ingrid arrived. Ingrid had just joined Else at a table when Rita came back from the dance floor and introduced the young man she had been dancing with.

"I'd like you to meet Erich. He works in the accounting department on third floor."

"Won't you join us," Else invited him.

The band struck up a waltz, and Erich asked Ingrid to dance.

"Oh, I haven't danced in years . . ."

"Well, I'll forgive you if you step on my toes, and I'll try not to step on yours."

With that, Erich led Ingrid off to the dance floor.

A few days later, Erich stopped by Ingrid's desk and asked her to go to a movie. Ingrid declined. A few days later, Erich asked her again. He was persistent. He kept on asking, and Ingrid finally accepted his invitation. They started to spend more and more time together going to movies, going for walks, and gradually a deep friendship developed. Erich was sincere, and Ingrid was able to trust him.

When Erich declared his love for her, Ingrid told him the complete story of Harry and baby Robert.

"Thank you for telling me. I knew about the baby from your friends, but not about Harry. You've had a lot to deal with on your own in the past. For me, the past is just that, the past. I love you now, and we can have a good future together. The future can be ours," Erich said, trying to assure Ingrid.

Ingrid allowed herself to listen to her feelings. It was as if all her sadness and sorrow had been lifted since Erich had become her friend. She realized that for some time now he had been more than just a friend, even though she had denied her feelings. They became engaged and married a year later.

Ingrid had finally found a man she could love and trust. The man she wanted to share her life with. Their happiness and their family were complete when they were blessed with a boy and later a girl.

Time passed. First, their son, and then their daughter were married. Ingrid and Erich were empty-nesters who enjoyed life and each other.

On December 21, 1985, Ingrid and Erich went out to an orchard to buy some apples for the upcoming Christmas holidays. Getting home late in the afternoon, Erich felt tired and decided to lie down for a while on the living room sofa. Ingrid went into the kitchen to get out some bread, cold cuts and cheeses for the customary light evening meal.

When she came back into the living room, Erich was barely alive. He had suffered a heart attack. Ingrid quickly called an ambulance, but when Erich arrived at the hospital he was pronounced dead.

Ingrid was devastated. She had lost her soul mate. Life without him seemed empty. It took a long time for Ingrid to adjust to life without Erich.

Several years after her husband's death, Ingrid and two of her friends flew to London for a week's vacation. While Ingrid told Mariele about the places they visited and the nice time they had, Harry's name was never mentioned. Perhaps Ingrid had found closure to that part of her life earlier. Mariele did not ask.

Ingrid still lives in her beloved Munich, and it is always a special day for her when her children and her granddaughter come to visit. She revels in her current joys, but there is a part of her past she never forgets. Every year on November 1, All Saints Day, Ingrid takes flowers to her husband's grave in Munich. Then she takes the S-Bahn to the suburb where she, Mariele, and I used to live and walks to the cemetery to bring a bouquet of flowers to her little Bobby.

Chapter 24

Dancing With the Enemy

The Occupation troops had settled into their various peacekeeping activities. At first, a no-fraternization order had been set up. It did not work. Realizing its failure, the authorities relaxed the order to where soldiers could speak to Germans in public places. The result was not much better.

Finally General Patton, Commander of the 3rd Army, suggested holding organized public dances that German girls could attend as invited guests.

The two units stationed in our vicinity wasted no time to make the necessary arrangements to find a site for their dances.

The U.S. Army Signal Corps, Frank's unit, was stationed in the former Dornier aircraft factory. They planned to hold dances at the ballroom of the nearby Bart Restaurant. The Quartermaster Company, stationed a few miles away in the next suburb, reserved the ballroom of another restaurant and called it the Casanova Club.

The units took turns hosting a dance every Saturday.

My friend Ralph had been sent back to the United States, so Frank invited me to come along to the first dance at Bart's with him and Mariele. I still remember how excited I was to go to a "real dance" in a ballroom, instead of dancing in our hallway to the records Mariele had brought with her from the United States almost eight years ago.

I was elated as we entered the ballroom. It was nicely decorated, and a band was setting up. We would be dancing to a live band. The dance was well-attended. We had barely sat down at a table when a GI came over and asked me for the first dance.

All evening I did not lack for dance partners. I felt like I was in a dream. While I danced with different GIs, Frank didn't give anyone a chance to dance with Mariele. He was truly smitten with her.

The next weekend we went to the dance at the Casanova Club. It was equally well-decorated, and we had an equally good time. For Mariele and me, the Saturday dances became the high point of the week.

The Valentine's Day dance at the Signal Corps was coming up, but Frank was on a detail to drive to Nuremberg that particular weekend. He would not be back for the dance. I did not want to miss that dance. When I was dancing, I felt young, alive, and carefree. Valentine's Day was unknown in Germany then, but Mariele told me what a special dance this was going to be. She said the ballroom would probably be decorated with hearts, flowers, cupids, and other Valentine symbols.

Well, I was determined not to miss it, so when two of the GIs at Military Government, where Mariele and I worked, asked us if we would go to the dance with them, I quickly accepted for Mariele and me. When I told Mariele about our dates on the way home, she wasn't sure that she wanted to go without Frank, but I soon convinced her that we didn't want to miss this dance. After all, she was the one who had told me how special Valentine's Day was.

Two days later, on our way home from work, two other GIs asked us if they might escort us to the dance. I had not seen or spoken to the soldiers from work with whom we had made the date earlier in the week, so we also accepted this invitation.

Getting to this dance was my number one priority. All week long at work I was dreaming about the dance and debating what to wear. Thanks to Aunt Katherine's packages, Mariele and I had some nice dresses for the dances.

I had just finished getting ready for the dance and wondering if our dates would show up, when the doorbell rang, and the GIs from work came to pick us up. I asked them in and ushered them into the living room, where we would wait for Mariele.

We were visiting when the doorbell rang again, and there were the two soldiers we had met on our way home. As I went to the door to answer the doorbell, my parents asked what was going on. I told them to please let me explain later.

The four soldiers and I were visiting. I had just told them that some of my girlfriends would be at the dance when Mariele arrived, but she was not alone. Frank had come back and brought along a buddy that had been on the same detail. So now there were six GIs. Frank was upset. He correctly assumed that I might have had something to do with these multiple dates.

"Just who is it you're going to the dance with?" Frank glared.

"Well, some of my girlfriends are probably already waiting to meet us at the dance. So, let's just all go."

With that I led the procession out of the living room and into the street.

At the end of our block, we met Else and Frieda, who were headed to the dance, but so far had no way to get in because they had no escorts. I introduced them and invited them to join us, and they did. I breathed a sigh of relief.

At the dance, the other two GIs had no problem finding dancing partners, and the night was saved.

The dancehall, decorated appropriately for Valentine's Day, looked beautiful. Mariele had certainly not exaggerated. The band had just started to play. We sat down at one of the tables and soon we were dancing, talking, and drinking rum and Cokes. The new dance craze was the jitterbug, a fast and energetic dance unknown in Germany.

Bob, the soldier I had been dancing with, offered to teach me. The jitterbug was lots of fun. We sat down to catch our breath, and Bob offered me a cigarette. I had tried some of Ludwig's cigarettes before the war, and I had gotten sick. But that was long ago, so I took the cigarette. These were American cigarettes; maybe they tasted better.

While I didn't really like it, this time I didn't get sick. So besides starting to jitterbug, I also started to smoke.

When the band took a break, sandwiches and cake were served as a special treat. We were famished and enjoyed the snacks. Then the band struck up again, and we were back out on the dance floor.

The evening went fast and all too soon they called for the last dance of the evening.

The next day at breakfast came the dreaded discussion with my parents. I got a stern lecture from my parents, especially Mama.

"Lately you think you can't live without dancing," Mama chastised me. "There is no excuse for making all of those dates. Why, one of those soldiers could have pulled his gun and killed all of us. Remember, they are, after all, the Occupation troops, and we are still the enemy they conquered."

I opened my mouth to make some lame excuse, but Mama didn't give me a chance.

"Aside from that, we did not bring you up to act that way. Show some character or maybe you'll stay home and think about it in the future."

There was not much I could say. Deep down, I knew she was right. I never made any more "insurance dates" after that.

Not only were my parents upset with me, Frank, too, was rather cool to me for a long time. But since I was Mariele's cousin, he still asked me to go to dances at both clubs with them.

"Saturday, Frank and I are going to the dance at the Casanova Club," Mariele told me. "He said you could come along."

"Yes, I'd love to go," I answered.

Saturday, Mariele and Frank picked me up and together the three of us walked to the Casanova Club. Once there, we were talking and having a good time in between dances, when a tall sergeant with wavy dark hair and a twinkle in his eyes came over and asked me to dance. He kept me out on the dance floor for the next several dances. He was a good dancer, and we danced well together.

When intermission was announced, we went back to the table. Bill, my dancing partner, introduced himself to Frank and asked if he might join us at the table. Frank introduced himself and Mariele, then invited him to join us. As usual, the conversation turned to Mariele and her perfect English.

When Bill referred to Mariele as my friend, I quickly corrected him:

"Mariele and I are cousins. Our grandmother, aunt and cousin Joey live in New York," I volunteered. "Where do you live, Bill?"

"I'm from Iowa," he answered.

"I've never heard of Iowa. Where is that?"

"Do you know where the Mississippi is?"

"Oh, yes, I've read about the Mississippi and the Wild West. That's where the Indians live, and huge herds of buffalo roam on the prairie."

"Well, the West isn't that wild anymore," chuckled Bill. "Iowa is the first state west of the Mississippi, and we're quite civilized now."

When there was rapid conversation going on, I had trouble understanding, and Mariele had to help out and translate, but we really had a good time. Bill was easy to talk with, and he made me laugh.

When the dance was over, Bill offered to drive us home in his Jeep, and we gladly accepted. As I unlocked the garden gate and told Bill good night, he asked if he could take me to the next dance.

"I'd be glad to also pick up your cousin and Frank, and we could go together, if that's OK with you."

From then on, the four of us started riding to the dances in Bill's Jeep.

"They are showing movies several times a week at the post. Would you like to see an American movie?" Bill asked Mariele and me a few weeks later.

"Would I ever! I haven't seen an American movie for over eight years," Mariele answered.

I, too, was immediately interested. We decided it would be nice to go on Friday night, a nice conclusion of the work week.

I did not always understand the rapid dialogue, but I found out some unique things about the American lifestyle. I remember one scene in particular. It showed a living room with teens lying on the carpet, reading. This would never happen in Germany. We always sat on chairs or perhaps lay on the sofa to read. I don't remember me or any of my friends ever lying on the floor to read or write. We enjoyed the movies, and now we looked forward to the Friday night movies as well as the Saturday night dances.

It was Saturday again, and I was waiting for Bill to pick me up for the dance. When he came, he had a mischievous grin on his face and said he had a surprise. As I walked out through the garden gate, there stood his Jeep, with my name, *Anneliese,* printed in bold letters on the front panel of the Jeep. I knew immediately Mama would not be happy.

Here I am with my handsome GI boyfriend and his Jeep,
which he named Anneliese.

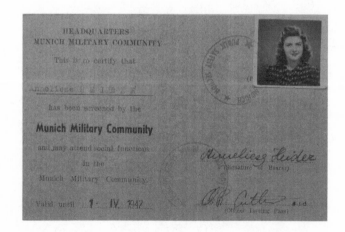

This is my Munich Military Social Pass,
which allowed me to go to dances with my GI boyfriend.

Mama and Papa liked Bill, but they would have liked it better if I didn't have a steady date. After all, Frank escorted both Mariele and me into the dance, and once there I could dance with whoever was there.

Mama reminded me that these soldiers would be leaving soon. It was best not to get attached to anyone in particular. While Mama quite openly voiced her hope that in time I would date and marry someone she and Papa knew, someone like one of Ludwig's friends, Papa was not quite as vocal about their future plans for me.

Bill started a little bartering with Mama. Bill liked the fresh fruit and vegetables from our garden. He especially liked Mama's green onions. In thanks for the fresh produce, he often brought Mama some real coffee. After dances we were usually hungry and a group of us often cooked raw fried potatoes with green onions, bacon, and eggs and had coffee—real coffee—before we ended the evening.

Bill and Frank were eager to see some of the beautiful Bavarian countryside. Sometimes on Sundays, when the weather was good, they, Mariele, and I started to go on daytrips. We visited the castles built by King Ludwig II, took the cable car up the *Zugspitze,* Bavaria's tallest mountain, and traveled to other attractions.

We all were spending more and more of our free time together. Sometimes Bill and Frank stopped by during the week after Mariele and I got home from work to play a board game or cards.

"I think you are seeing too much of Bill," Mama voiced her concern. "Remember, one of these days he will be going back to the States."

Mama was too late. Bill and I were in love. Bill had earlier signed up to extend his stay of duty, but that, too, was coming to an end. I had closed my mind to the fact that no matter what the outcome would be, I would be hurt.

So far, we were still the enemy. No peace treaty had been signed, nor would it be signed in the near future. Would Bill write, like he had told me, or would I, like Ingrid and many German girls who fell in love with a soldier, never hear from him again? Even if he kept his promise and asked me to marry him, could I leave my parents, Ludwig, and Germany?

Dancing with the enemy had started out almost accidentally. It had brought good times and love, but it also brought unforeseen problems that would eventually necessitate making painful decisions.

Chapter 25

Military Government for Bavaria

If you do not know another language,
you do not know your own.

—Goethe

The Office of Military Government for Bavaria had been set up in Munich in the *Tegernseerlandstrasse* in the former *Werkzeugmeisterei*, Supply Depot, for the German Army. Because there were not nearly enough qualified interpreters available within the Military Government, they had to rely on us, the conquered enemy, to interpret for them.

After the Allied victory, I had returned to work in the offices of the German railroad near my home, and Mariele was again at work at the Bavarian Ministry of Food and Agriculture. During a meeting when Mariele interpreted between the Bavarian Ministry and Military Government, Colonel J. C. of the Military Government was so impressed with her fluency in English that he hired her on the spot, and in June 1945 Mariele began her new job as interpreter. She was delighted with her new job. Interpreting gave her the opportunity to make use of her English language skills.

It was a sad day in the late summer of 1946 for Mariele and me when first Frank, and a few months later Bill, were sent back to the United States. We both were very much in love with our American boyfriends and had accepted their proposals before they left. We hoped that we would be able to join them in America to be married. Fortunately for us, we had our jobs to keep us busy during the day, but the evenings without Frank and Bill seemed empty, and we anxiously awaited that first letter.

Unfortunately, we soon had different concerns.

In the late fall of 1946, Mariele's mother was diagnosed with breast cancer and needed radical surgery. Mariele took an extensive leave of absence and, upon Mariele's recommendation, Colonel J.C. hired me to fill in for her.

I quit my job with the railroad and in the weeks until her mother's surgery, Mariele kept working to introduce me to my duties within the Office of Military Government. After the surgery, Mariele stayed at home to take care of her mother and the household. I was on my own.

Because public transportation and many of the rail lines were still in the process of being repaired, I took the train only as far as Pasing every morning. There a truck from Military Government transported me and other "German nationals," as we were called, the rest of the way to work. After a thorough check by the MPs, we were allowed to enter the gate into building, which was surrounded by barbed wire.

I thought it ironic that they searched me and my purse, but they could not search my mind. I actually could have interpreted anything I wanted to.

I wanted the job in the worst way, but felt totally inadequate following in Mariele's footsteps. I was deliriously happy and panic-stricken at the same time: deliriously happy to have the job, panic-stricken at my obvious lack of fluency in English. I carried my English-German dictionary under my arm like it was another appendage to my body.

The pay at Military Government was not great, but that did not matter because there was very little we could buy with German money. The shelves in the stores were empty. American cigarettes and "real"coffee were the new currency that could be traded for butter, flour, oil, meat, and other necessities.

The advantage of my work at Military Government was that the civilian staff was allowed to eat lunch in the commissary along with the GIs and other employees. While some of the Americans complained about the beef hash, canned peaches, fruit cocktail, Spam, canned vegetables, and other typical commissary foods, to me it was manna from heaven, for which I didn't even have to give up any of my precious food stamps.

Every day we had a slice of beautiful white bread on our tray. This I always put in a little brown bag to take home to Mama. Getting a full meal at my job meant more food for us at home. The biggest bonus of all was an extra youth ration card I received at work every month.

I was immersed in the English language all day long and found my language skills growing tremendously. Colonel J.C. was very patient with my limited English. He was probably the most positive person I have ever met. He came sauntering into the office every morning, his jacket hooked over his shoulder:

"Good morning! It's a great day. Have the dispatches arrived?"

"Good morning, sir. They are sorted on your desk. Today, you also have a three-power meeting at 9:30."

"I'm afraid it'll be a waste of my time. As always, the U.S. and the Brits will agree on something, but the Russians will say, '*Nyet*, no,' and walk out," Colonel J.C. answered. But he always attended the meetings.

Odilia K. was a secretary to Colonel Q. on our floor. Her husband, Bart, worked in the motor pool for the Military Government. They had lived in Lithuania. Fearing the Russian onslaught, they escaped in the middle of the night, each carrying only two suitcases of their belongings, and fled to Germany. They were less afraid of the Germans than of the Russians.

Odilia was a very hard-working young woman, but when it was time to translate for a meeting with Russians in attendance, she would hide in the bathroom. Someone else had to go and translate in her place. She was still deathly afraid of the Russians. Whenever Russians were in the building, it was hard to find anyone from the

Eastern Zone around. That was a curious phenomenon, but one I understood, given the fear that we ourselves had of the Russians.

In due time, Mariele's mother came home from the hospital, and Mariele took care of her for several weeks. When Mariele finally returned to work, I dreaded the thought of having to find another job, even though with my newly acquired English ability that should not have been too difficult.

The thought of losing the extra ration card and the noon meal was worse than the thought of losing the job. To my surprise, Colonel J.C. said they would keep me on to deal with the extra workload.

I consistently tried to pick up new words to increase my vocabulary whenever and wherever I got a chance. Next to the office where I worked was the room where the couriers brought in the dispatches. I could not help but overhear their conversations and often picked up new words. This was not the smart thing to do, as I soon found out.

Colonel J.C.'s wife, as well as the wives of some of the other officers, had arrived from the States. Because we would sometimes have to accompany the officers' wives and interpret for them, a welcome dinner was given for the wives. Mariele and I were to attend the dinner so the wives could meet us.

That evening I had been listening but had not said much. I felt I should contribute something to the conversation so during a lull in the conversation, I decided it was time to use some of my new vocabulary.

"I really got pissed today, when my typewriter" . . . is all that I got out before my cousin, who was sitting next to me, clamped her hand on my forearm, saying:

"Please, excuse us," then ordered me, "Come along." We proceeded to the restroom. Once inside, she angrily demanded: "Do you know what you just said?"

"One of the drivers used it, and I could tell it means that you are really, really mad, so I decided to try it out . . . ."

"Well, it's not a word for you to use," and she proceeded to explain its meaning. "Don't you ever again use words you don't know. Ask me first. Now go back and apologize."

"There's no way I'm going back in there. I can't face all of those people."

"Yes, you will. You have to go back to work on Monday, so you better get it done now. Let's go."

Back at the table I apologized and explained that I was trying to learn more English and had listened to one of the drivers. For a moment there was stunned silence, then Colonel J.C. laughed as he explained: "Unfortunately, you won't learn the best English if you listen to some of our drivers. Better stick to your dictionary."

Everyone seemed to be in agreement. The situation became relaxed again, and when even Mariele managed a smile, I felt my distress eased. I apparently had been forgiven my *faux pas*.

I may have been forgiven, but it was not forgotten.

After Colonel and Mrs. J. C. returned to the United States, they stayed in contact with Mariele and me and we became good friends. Over the years, when I visited with them on the phone or in person, my dinner *faux pas* would come back to haunt me.

Colonel J.C. or his wife would sometimes ask, "Anneliese, have you learned any new words lately?" and we would laugh about that long-ago incident. My *faux pas* became one of the mutually shared episodes that bound us together until their deaths a few years ago.

But to return to our experiences as translators, I have to say that sometimes even Mariele found herself challenged in her translating.

In particular, I remember one such circumstance which occurred after Mariele had come back from her leave. She was assigned to interpret for Colonel Q., who unlike Colonel J.C., was not an easy person to work for. He was quite open in his extreme dislike for anything German, especially the people.

In this case, an elderly German official had come into Colonel Q's office, clicked his heels, thinking it was correct to do so in a military post. At this Colonel Q. shouted, "I don't want to deal with him" and started cursing in the worst way.

Mariele was at a loss and finally told him:

"Sir, I'm sorry, I don't know how to translate all of these curse words. I am translating that you said many curse words, that you do not wish to deal with him because you were offended at his heel clicking and that he was to leave."

Mariele was ever so relieved when the man left, and she was dismissed to go back to Colonel J.C.'s office.

Another challenge in my English language progress presented itself after that first long-awaited letter from Bill arrived. He wrote that his troop transport ship had taken 12 days to cross the ocean and that other discharge formalities took more time before he finally was on the train for his home in Iowa. He was now in the process of getting the necessary paperwork started so I would be allowed to come to the United States to join him.

Now it was my turn to write letters to Bill. I only knew office correspondence. My love letters were more like business letters, rather stiff and formal. I begged Mariele to help me. She wrote the most beautiful letters, and so we would sit down together and write our love letters.

I copied some of Mariele's letters almost word for word. I thought what she wrote could not be improved upon; I knew I could not express my thoughts any better. It was a learning experience of a different kind. It's a good thing Frank and Bill lived so far apart. Neither Mariele nor I ever told them the story of our love letters.

Before we were to leave for the United States, Colonel and Mrs. J.C. invited us to dinner at their home in the Munich Military Compound. As well as a farewell dinner, they also wanted us to see what it was like to entertain in the United States. In Germany during the war, we never had friends or neighbors over for dinner or even coffee.

Mrs. J.C. was serving dessert, ice cream, something we had not had in a long time. She casually mentioned that she had planned to make a cake but just didn't feel like it.

While we loved the ice cream, we really couldn't figure out why one wouldn't feel like making a cake when there were obviously plenty of ingredients available. It just didn't make sense to us. It had been drilled into us that you did what you needed to do, and how you felt or how tired you were did not matter.

On April 1, 1947, Mariele and I resigned our jobs at Munich Military Government in preparation for going to the United States to be married to our fiancés.

In order to immigrate to the United States, we had to provide the necessary documents to the American Consulate. One of them was our *denazification* card showing that we had not been active in the Nazi Party. Both Mariele and I fell under the *Jugendamnestie*, youth amnesty, because of our youth during the war. I received my youth amnesty on my 19th birthday. We also had to have complete physicals.

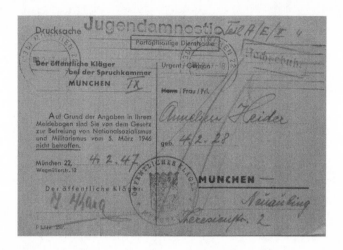

This is my denazification card,
which I received on my 19th birthday.

Meanwhile, in the United States, our future husbands had to fill out many forms, provide for our airline tickets, and deposit funds which they would get back only after we were married. This was so that we could be returned to Germany in case they left us stranded.

All these preliminary items had to be sent to the American Consulate. For us, there were endless trips to the U.S. Consulate and hours of waiting. The U.S. authorities didn't make it easy for us to get to the United States.

Finally, we were notified that all of our papers were in order, and we were to leave on a flight with American Overseas Airlines on Friday, June 13th, 1947, for New York City.

Now we had to start packing. Aunt Katherine's wooden ships' trunks, which had been stored in our attic, were brought down and thoroughly cleaned. Things that had been given to me for my trousseau over the years, mainly before the war, were packed.

Mama felt badly because she had always thought what a wonderful trousseau she and Papa would provide for me, yet now there was nothing they could buy. Mama gave me a white damask tablecloth and napkins she had bought before the war, and our seamstress put my monogram in the corner of each napkin.

I picked a few of my favorite books, my photo albums, a green-and-gold, hand-painted china coffee set, the ebony and silver crucifix my parents had given me, my *Sammeltassen,* a crystal vase from Friedl, and a crystal fruit bowl from my godmother, Julie.

I sorted through my clothes. The summer things I would take with me in the two large suitcases I was allowed to take on the plane. My winter clothing would have to go into the trunks. We packed and repacked until the two trunks were considered ready for their long journey across the ocean.

This picture was taken in June 1947, on the last day Mariele and I were in Germany. From left: Papa; Mama; me; my cousin Mariele's mother, Aunt Marie; Mariele; and Mariele's father, Uncle Willie.

My cousin Mariele (left) and me. We were called
"Night and Day" because Mariele was blonde,
and I was brunette.

Chapter 26

Only in America

Friday, June 13, 1947. Our plane has just taken off from Frankfurt Airport and is now gaining altitude. In the seat next to me is my cousin Mariele. We are both German war brides.

As I look down, the bombed-out ruins of the city stare back at me like the empty eye sockets of a skull. My mind automatically associates aircraft with raining death and destruction from the sky. This plane is different. It is taking me to Bill, the man I am going to marry, to my new home and my new country, America. I am nineteen years old.

Saying good-bye to Mama and Papa was the hardest thing I have ever done. I had to walk away from our house in the suburbs of Munich that had provided a happy home when my brother, Ludwig, and I were children and had sheltered my parents and me during the long, terrifying war years.

Ludwig was still a prisoner of war in Russia. I wouldn't be there when he comes home . . . if he does . . . . The Russians have yet to release most of their prisoners. I was torn between my family and the man I love. I had made my decision, but that did not ease the hurt deep inside me. Will I ever see any of them again?

We have our first glimpse of the English Channel below, when we feel the plane turn. Soon, there is an announcement that we are returning to Frankfurt because of motor trouble. In Frankfurt, we are allowed to stay on the plane, and it isn't very long before we are airborne again. We are flying across the English Channel, headed for Shannon, Ireland.

Mariele and I stand in front of the American Overseas
Airlines plane that will take us to America. We dressed
for the occasion, in hats and silver fox furs.

"I'm so glad we were able to get on the same plane," I tell Mariele. "It will be hard for me when I have to go on to Iowa without you."

"You'll do just fine, and remember we'll be able to call each other. Almost everyone in the States has a phone," she consoles me.

Mariele is lucky. Her parents are planning to return to the United States as soon as possible. My parents promised to come and visit me, but it may be a long time before they can get permission to travel. First of all, Ludwig has to come home.

After landing in Shannon, Ireland, we deplane only briefly. But back on the tarmac, ready for take-off, we hear the announcement that everyone is to disembark and proceed to the terminal. Engine trouble again. I feel uneasy. Neither Mariele nor I have ever flown before and while I am not superstitious, it *is* Friday, the 13th! Is this an omen for my future in America?

The passengers disembarking are mainly wives and dependants of military personnel returning to the States. As far as we can determine Mariele and I are the only German war brides on the plane.

At Shannon Airport, we are ushered into a room where a buffet table with sandwiches, salads, cookies, and other items has been set up for us. After helping ourselves to some food, we sit down at a small table. A waiter comes to check if we would like anything else. It is a warm and muggy night, so we ask for something cold to drink. We have had very little to eat since we left Munich, and the food and sodas refresh us.

To our embarrassment, the waiter comes back with a bill for the sodas. Being "alien war brides," we are not allowed to carry American currency, and German money is of no value. We are literally without a penny.

Since hot coffee and tea were on the buffet table, we had assumed that cold beverages were also included. Explaining our situation, we offer to send the money as soon as we arrive in the States. The waiter is very kind, but declines our offer. He tells us not to worry, it will be taken care of.

By now we feel as if all of the other passengers are staring at us, and we are totally humiliated by our financial insufficiency. What a way to start out.

It is well after midnight when we finally leave Shannon for the long flight across the ocean.

For Mariele, to land in New York will be like a homecoming. She has lived in New York for ten years, knows most of the relatives there, and speaks and writes the language fluently.

For me, New York is a strange city, and the only person besides Mariele that I will know is my maternal grandmother, *Grossmama*. But I have not seen her since before the war. That was when she left for New York to visit her daughter Katherine, whom I barely remember from her visit with us in Germany when I was four years old.

When we arrive at the airport in New York City, people around us speak English so fast that I can't understand a word. Finally, Mariele and I are finished with customs and go out to the visitors' area where

Aunt Katherine, Uncle Joe, and Mariele's fiancé, Frank, are waiting for us.

My fiancé, Bill, had written me that he would not be able to meet me in New York. However, I feel sure that that was a little white lie because he wants to surprise me. But as I look around, I don't see him. I suddenly feel totally alone amid all the welcoming around me. It is hard to hide my disappointment.

Our first stop is Frank's mother's house, where Frank's whole extended family has congregated for a delicious meal with a great variety of Italian dishes and several bottles of wine. The conversation is flowing and is so animated that it seems as though everyone is talking at the same time. Mariele and I are told over and over how happy they are that we have finally arrived. What a great welcome! But these people are our family and friends. How will strangers react to us? No peace treaty with Germany has been signed. Legally, we are still the enemy. Will our new country accept us?

It is late in the afternoon when we drive to Aunt Katherine's home where I finally meet my cousin Joey. Even though he is two years younger, he is taller than I am. He is handsome, with dark wavy hair and a happy smile. We hit it off immediately.

Grossmama looks a lot older than I remember her, but then why shouldn't she? It has been ten years since I last saw her. In spite of the lapse in time and the distance that had separated us, we greet each other warmly and renew our bonds of relationship.

At dinnertime no one is hungry, so we have a light snack and something to drink. It has been a long trip and a full and exciting, but exhausting, day. Mariele and I are grateful when Aunt Katherine shows us to the downstairs bedroom and bathroom we are to share. Cousin Joey has already placed our luggage in the room. We unpack only what we need for the night. Even though we are tired, it does take us a while to unwind and get to sleep.

The next morning, I awaken to the radio playing a song about shining shoes with Shinola. Puzzled, I look at Mariele.

"That's a commercial. Companies pay to have their products advertised on the radio," Mariele explains.

"You mean Aunt Katherine doesn't have to pay five marks for each radio, like we did in Germany?"

"That's right."

"Gee, that's pretty neat."

"We better get ready for breakfast. I remember Aunt Katherine doesn't like to wait for people when it comes to mealtime."

Grossmama and Aunt Katherine are already at the breakfast table. Uncle Joe had left for work earlier, and Cousin Joey was at his summer job. He is earning money for college, I'm told.

Breakfast is another surprise. The butter is salted. Why put salted butter on bread and then put sweet jelly or honey over it? What a waste of precious butter.

After breakfast, Aunt Katherine asks Mariele and me to follow her as she heads downstairs, razor in hand. She takes us into the bathroom and proceeds to tell us:

"As I told you yesterday, we're having a cook-out today. All of our relatives, as well as some of our German friends, want to meet you. In America, we shave under our arms and our legs. Here is a razor. You better shave before our guests arrive."

I was relieved. For a fleeting moment when Aunt Katherine, a stranger to me until yesterday, started down the stairs with a razor, I thought back to Germany. After the war, sometimes girls who dated "Amis," American soldiers, were attacked and had their heads shaved. But I was in America now, and even though I thought only call girls and movie stars shaved in Germany, I shaved.

About noon, the relatives begin to arrive. Every family brings something to eat. I can't believe my eyes. So many people and such an abundance of food. In Germany before the war, we sometimes had a few relatives in for special occasions, but never this many. We also did not have neighbors or friends over for dinner. Most often, relatives would be invited for cake and coffee or tea. Should people be invited for dinner, they would bring the hostess flowers, a box of chocolates, or a bottle of wine. Here, it seemed, the relatives and friends bring part of the meal.

Meeting all of the new relatives was overwhelming. The cousins about my age seemed so young, bubbly, and carefree. At nineteen, I felt oddly old and sober. I was in the middle of so many new and overwhelming impressions on that first day that it finally came to me what I had done and how far from home I really was. Everything was strange and foreign. Mariele was introducing Frank to all of the relatives, so I took refuge and talked in German with *Grossmama,* who knew even less English than I.

When it was time to eat, one of Uncle Joe's nephews, Ben, followed me to the food table and explained the different foods to me, then took a seat next to me at one of the tables. For the rest of the party, he didn't leave my side. He was polite, nice looking and seemed sure of himself. Home from college, he had been admitted to law school. He, too, had a summer job. He was careful to speak slowly, and it was easy to listen to him.

After the guests had left, I was drained. None of Uncle Joe's relatives spoke German, so I had been speaking and listening to lots of different English speakers. I was mentally exhausted. Translating for the Military Government had been totally different. I was relieved to hear that tomorrow evening we were invited to Aunt Katherine and Uncle Joe's friends where we could talk German.

The next morning after breakfast another surprise awaited us. Aunt Katherine took us shopping. We went shopping in the car! Such luxury! The stores were full of merchandise, and there was such a great selection of goods in all sizes and colors it was confusing. Anything one could possibly want was available, and no one had to stand in line. The clerks were very friendly and didn't hurry us.

Aunt Katherine asked me to pick out a bedspread as a wedding present for Bill and me. I can still see it in my mind. It was white chenille, with the design of a big basket of flowers in pastel colors in the center and a border around the outside edge. The saleslady not only put the bedspread in a nice box with tissue paper and the store's name imprinted, but also put the box in a shopping bag, again with the store name in big letters. Such abundance, such luxury!

We came home with many shopping bags, and Uncle Joe took our picture to commemorate our first shopping trip in the United States—another almost dreamlike experience.

When we arrived home, Ben and Joey were outside throwing a big round ball into a net, which had a hole in the bottom. They told me they were shooting baskets. Ben had come to pick up the jacket he forgot at the barbeque. We sat in the yard and talked. Before Ben left, he asked me if I would go to a movie with him. I told him I didn't think I should; I was engaged to be married.

"Yes, I know, but you're not married yet."

Mariele (left), Aunt Katherine, and I pose with our packages
after our first shopping trip in New York City.

Five of us pause during a welcome party held for us at the
home of Aunt Katherine's friends in New York. From left:
Aunt Katherine, me, Uncle Joe, Cousin Joey, and Mariele.

I was confused. Was he trying to date me? Or was he just being nice because I was his friend's cousin? I told him that I was tired from the shopping, which was true.

The next day, Aunt Katherine took us along to the grocery store, again by car. It seems everyone drove a car. I didn't see any bicycles. In the few days I had been in the United States, I'd had more rides in a car than in all the years I lived in Germany.

Not only were the store shelves full, but there also were different brands of everything and various sizes of each brand. No one cared how many things one bought. At the checkout counter, a young man who was just standing around started to take our groceries. I quickly reached for them, but Aunt Katherine stopped me, laughed, and said: "He's just going to carry them out to the car. That's his job."

I couldn't believe it. Not only do they let you buy whatever you want, and provide bags for everything, but they even carry the bags to your car. Only in America . . . .

I also was struck by the fact there were no fences in Aunt Katherine and Uncle Joe's neighborhood, and during the day the house door was not locked. Such openness and trust!

In just a few days, I was living in a totally different world. I wanted to tell Mama and Papa and wished they could be here to experience this life so far removed from fear and the aftermath of a long and devastating war.

I sat down and wrote them a long letter pouring out my initial impressions of life in America.

One afternoon after Uncle Joe came home from work, he announced: "Let's not waste this beautiful afternoon. Get ready. We are going to Coney Island."

Joey also invited a girl from his class and Ben to come along. Mariele's fiancé, Frank, came to pick up Mariele and in two cars we headed out for Coney Island.

After arriving, Uncle Joe stopped at an ice cream vendor's stand. "Well, Anneliese, how many scoops do you want?" I didn't understand *scoops*. Pointing to an advertisement of an ice cream cone he gestured: "Ice cream, how high? Three, four, five?"

Ice cream was something we hadn't had for years, so I said, "Five high."

"You heard the young lady. She wants an ice cream cone 'five high.' Can you do it?"

"I can sure try," was the amused vendor's reply.

We all watched as he skillfully piled five scoops on a big cone, and everyone was laughing as I carefully balanced my "five high" ice cream cone. The ice cream vendor handed Uncle Joe a paper cup, "just in case," he laughed.

We had lots of fun. Ben stuck to me like flies to a glue strip, and I did enjoy all the attention he gave me. People seemed so carefree and happy that their joy was infectious.

After a while, Uncle Joe told us the fireworks would start soon, and we went to find a seat. The display of colors was spectacular, but the loud explosions reminded us of other times, and unwilling tears were streaming down Mariele's and my face.

Uncle Joe and Aunt Katherine realized the fireworks were too much for us, and so we left halfway through the display.

Frank and Mariele went to see a late movie. They asked if I'd like to go along, but I declined. I knew they would like some time to themselves. When we got back to Aunt Katherine's, Joey said he had something to do. That left Ben and me.

"I wish you'd stay a little longer in New York," Ben urged. "I'm home from college all summer. We could get to know each other."

"Ben, I really like you, but . . . ."

"When I saw you, it was love at first sight for me. Please stay and let me date you."

"I am engaged. I already have a ticket to fly to Iowa."

"Just give me a chance. Come to dinner with my parents tomorrow. After dinner, we'll take in a movie. I'll call you."

After Ben left, Aunt Katherine said:

"Ben sure has been around a lot. I think he's smitten with you."

"He knows I'm engaged and will be leaving for Iowa . . . ."

"That's just it. We know nothing about Bill or his family. I was disappointed that Bill didn't come to New York to meet you and us. Your Uncle Joe and I had invited him."

"I was disappointed, too, but he wrote me that it was not possible for him to get away just now."

But deep down, I wondered what could be so important to keep him away. I, too, had wanted for Bill to meet my New York family. Aunt Katherine was still talking, . . .

"Ben is a nice young man. He comes from a good family, and we sure would like to have you close by. I only hope Bill takes good care of you and provides for you."

"He loves me. I'm sure he will . . . . Please excuse me. It's been a great day, thank you for everything. I am really tired. I think I'd like to go to bed and read till Mariele gets back."

I needed to get away, be by myself. I got ready for bed, but I couldn't sleep. The truth was I wanted to go to the movies with Ben. I enjoyed being with him, I enjoyed being with him too much.

Do I have feelings for Ben? This is ridiculous, I don't even know him . . . . But how much do I know about Bill? . . . Only what he told me . . . . Frank's family welcomed Mariele with open arms . . . . Bill called me twice while I was here in New York. There had not been a single word of welcome from his family.

I had been so sure of my love for Bill. Now I was confused. But I made a decision. When Ben called the next day, I told him that I could not come to dinner, and I could not see him again.

After nine days in New York, I packed my suitcases. My thoughts turned to Iowa. Once I arrived there, I knew I would have only my future husband to turn to.

Chapter 27

Iowa

Aunt Katherine, Uncle Joe, and Mariele took me to the airport. Saying good-bye to them was so difficult that it took all my composure to put on a good front, to smile, and suppress the tears that wanted to well up in my eyes.

Mariele had been like my sister and my best friend through all of the oppressive war years. Now we would be separated. When it was time to say good-bye, it would not have taken much for me to stay in New York.

My flight had been called, and I walked out to the plane and up the stairs. I turned around and waved one last time just before I boarded the plane. I was on my own now, on the way to Iowa, to Bill.

Looking down on the towns and cities, I saw how peaceful they appeared. They were all intact, not bombed-out shells and rat-infested ruins like the cities in Europe. Even though I had been a good student in geography while I was in school and I had checked out the route on the map, I was amazed at how large this country was. I felt we had been flying forever, but when we landed we were only in Chicago to take on more passengers.

Once we left Chicago, we were on the last leg of the flight to Des Moines, the capital of Iowa, where Bill was going to meet me. Looking down from the plane, I was intrigued to see so much wide open land, not city upon city. I saw a river snaking its way through the landscape. Even though it didn't match its reputation from up above, I knew this must be the mighty Mississippi. The stewardess confirmed this.

I smiled as I thought back to the time when I read about the Mississippi in Ludwig's Karl May books. Reading about Winnetou and Old Shatterhand, the Mississippi and the American West had been my escape during the long war years. It was two years ago that the war ended, but dark memories lingered, and I wondered about my brother, Ludwig, who was still a prisoner in Russia.

I felt the plane descending. The stewardess announced that we were approaching the Des Moines airport and reminded the passengers to fasten the seat belts.

Iowa, Des Moines, and Bill. I was apprehensive now and wondered. *Is Bill as excited as I am? It's been such a long time since we kissed each other good-bye at the train station in Munich, when he said he would apply for a visa for me to come to the States so we could get married.* Then, for a moment, I panicked as I thought of Ingrid. *What if he isn't there to meet me? I'm going to be all alone in Iowa. I don't even know how to make a phone call.*

The plane's wheels touched ground and jolted me out of my thoughts. I looked out of the window and saw rain pelting down on the runway. Finally the "fasten seatbelts" sign went off, and the doors were opened. I got my carry-on down and waited in line to get off. After what seemed an eternity, I walked off the plane to the waiting area.

My heart was pounding. I stopped and looked around. There were so many people, all strangers, so many foreign voices . . . .

A man in a grey suit was rushing through the waiting crowd. It was Bill. I had never seen him in anything but his uniform. *He looks like a stranger to me . . . .* Then I felt his strong arms around me, and I smelled the familiar scent of his aftershave. He kissed me, and the months of separation didn't exist anymore. We both started laughing at the same time.

"Welcome to Iowa, honey, your new home west of the Mississippi," Bill said, and I knew I was home in my new country.

Epilogue

Stranger at the Gate

A little over a year after Mariele and I had left for the States, my parents experienced a startling and momentous event, and one that was recounted to me so often I feel as though I lived through it.

It was the summer of 1948, and although the war had ended in 1945, the times in Germany were still very hard. German money could not buy anything, the shelves in the stores were almost bare. I knew from information coming to me from various sources, and particularly from the letters I was receiving from my parents and friends, that all over Germany, cities were painstakingly being reclaimed from the rubble and devastation.

Like building materials, food was scarce and rationing cards were necessary for almost everything. People kept not only their house doors, but also their garden gates, locked at all times. Any available space in private homes was assigned to house the hundreds of thousands of refugees. My mother and father also had to share their home with strangers who had lost their home and everything during the air raids.

Even with a house full of people, Mama and Papa felt lonesome. Ludwig, their son, was their constant concern. The Russians freed their prisoners only sporadically and did not give out any information about the number of POWs still held by them or their names. The war had been over for more than three years and still my parents did not know whether Ludwig was still alive.

Mama and Papa took comfort in the letters they received from me, which, however, were not frequent enough to suit Mama. Whenever one arrived, it was a special day for them. It was even more special when there was a snapshot in the letter of our little boy, Larry. He was just about three months old now. In their letters, they wrote me how much they wished that they could see him, maybe even babysit him for a few hours. This was their first grandchild, and they ached to hold him in their arms.

From the letters my parents wrote, I understood that the fruit trees and the large garden they had planted promised a plentiful harvest, and I could imagine how the trees and the garden looked and what my mother's and father's days would be like. Mama would work in the garden and feed the chickens. Papa would take care of the rabbits after he got home from work.

On one particular day, which turned out to be the eventful day, Mama was in the kitchen, glad that she could sit down and read the newspaper, when the doorbell rang. She looked out the kitchen window down the long drive and saw a ragged looking man standing outside the gate. She opened the window and asked what he wanted.

"Don't you recognize me, Mama? It's me, Ludwig," an anxious, weary voice answered.

Mama couldn't believe it. There he was. "*Ja*, Ludwig, *ja*, Ludwig," she kept saying while she was running to the garden gate, tears streaming down her face, only to realize when she got there, that in the excitement she had forgotten to bring the keys to unlock the gate.

Returning to the house, she fetched the keys and let Ludwig in. He looked like a walking skeleton, haggard, sick, and emaciated. His clothes were dirty, and they hung on him. Instead of shoes, rags tied with twine were wrapped around his feet. He had left as a nineteen year old. Now, he looked much older that his twenty-eight years.

Mama kept crying and didn't know what to do first. Ludwig was very quiet and weary to the bone. She warmed up some of the soup left over from the noon meal. Ludwig was hungrily eating it, when Papa came home. There was another joyful reunion.

After Ludwig had finished the soup, Papa heated the stove in the bathroom so Ludwig could take a bath while Mama got out some clean clothes for him. Ludwig was exhausted and soon fell asleep at home and in his own bed.

Mama felt the terrible burden of uncertainty lift off her shoulders, and with the loss of that burden, she gained renewed strength.

Ludwig had been released because he had an abscess in his jaw and was no longer able to work. The Russians had shipped Ludwig and other prisoners of war across Russia to the German border in locked cattle cars. Several had died during the arduous journey. Dead or alive, the Russians could announce to the world that they had released a certain number of prisoners.

Mariele's Uncle Hans, a dentist, examined Ludwig's teeth. What was at first thought to be an infected tooth turned out to be much more. The infection had spread into the jaw bone and part of the bone had to be replaced with a metal plate.

This was not Ludwig's only health issue. Mama had to be very careful not to give Ludwig too much food, or food that was too rich for his system. He suffered from severe malnutrition and had open sores on his legs. By feeding him small quantities of nutritional food every few hours, she gradually nursed him back to health.

Three-and-a-half years after the war had ended, Mama and Papa finally had their first-born back, and their lives had new purpose.

It was a difficult decision for Ludwig to resume his studies. There were too many ghosts in his mind to be able to focus on studying, and there were many times he wanted to quit. Eventually his efforts were rewarded, and in December 1952, he graduated with a degree in engineering from the Technische Hochschule in Munich. He found a position with the German Postal Ministry and eventually rose to become *Oberpostrat,* an adviser to the postal minister.

Several years later, however, when he was offered the position of Postal Minister for the city of Berlin in the then-Russian-occupied zone, he declined. In no way did he want to go back anywhere near the Russian zone. He had too many dark memories.

For many years, Ludwig had the same nightmare. He was in the POW camp, and a truck had come to take the prisoners back to Germany. They all had to hurry and get to the truck, and he could not move fast enough, and the truck left without him.

Ludwig sits at home in my parents' orchard in Munich in
1948. He was a prisoner of war in Russia for more than
three-and-a-half years.

Mama and Papa beam with happiness. After nine years,
they have their son, Ludwig, back home.

Ludwig was satisfied to stay in Bonn until his death at age 82 in
the year 2002.

Postscript

The Cat Has Nine Lives—
Or, Why Didn't We Do Something?

After coming to the United States, I was often asked: "Why didn't people do something to stop Hitler?"

There was a strong civilian opposition to him, but what could be done when even the top military men and men who had political power could not succeed in assassinating the elusive dictator?

Thousands paid with their lives for their overt or covert resistance to the Third Reich. There was resistance. It had to be underground, but it was significant.

I do remember as a 10 year old that big war clouds hung over Europe in 1938. Hitler demanded the annexation of the Sudetenland area of Czechoslovakia to Germany. My parents and relatives were talking and worrying about the possibility of war. The general assumption was that the negotiations that were taking place in Munich in September 1938 were our last chance to avoid war.

Actually, our last chance was the Oster Conspiracy of 1938. Lieutenant Colonel Hans Oster of the *Abwehr*, the German Armed Forces Intelligence, and men from top military and state echelons were ready to kill Hitler should he go to war with Czechoslovakia over the Sudetenland.

The German diplomat Theodor Kordt from the German Embassy in London was the link to make sure the British would stand firm and condemn Hitler's demands to seize the Sudetenland area.

Neville Chamberlain from Britain, Edouard Daladier from France, and Benito Mussolini from Italy met with Hitler in Munich in September 1938. Czechoslovakia was not present; it had not been invited. After endless negotiations, Chamberlain gave in to the *Führer's* demands. All four signed the Munich Agreement on September 30, and the Sudetenland became part of Germany.

My parents, people in Germany and Europe, with the exception of Czechoslovakia, were jubilant. War was avoided. What none of them realized was that by appeasing the tyrant, war had become a certainty. The Munich Agreement destroyed any chance for the Oster plot to be carried out. Hitler went on to occupy Czechoslovakia, and, in September 1939, invaded Poland, beginning World War II.

Had the Oster conspiracy succeeded, World War II may have been averted and millions of people would have been spared violent and untimely death.

The Oster conspirators survived and became part of the German Resistance during World War II. But in 1945, it was discovered that Oster had conspired against Hitler since before the war, and Oster was hanged.

In 1939, before the war, General von Hammerstein and retired General Ludwig Beck repeatedly invited Hitler to inspect installations along the Siegfried Line, the German fortifications along the Rhine border, with the intention of assassinating him. Hitler never accepted the invitations.

German army officers were appalled by the outrageous crimes committed against the Jews and civilian population by the SS. This was not war; this was murder in the name of Germany. Many agreed to join the resistance.

One attempt to resist Hitler took place during the victory parade in Paris on July 27, 1940. Count Fritz-Dietlov von der Schulenberg was to shoot Hitler while Hitler was viewing the troops during the parade. But on July 20, Hitler cancelled the parade.

There would be three more attempts on Hitler's life in Paris alone. Hitler either canceled appointments, came early, or left early, each time foiling any attempt at assassination.

I remember how one attempt to resist Hitler intersected with my life. It was a cold day in February 1943. Mama was getting breakfast ready, so Papa and I could catch the train to get to work.

"Anneliese, hurry and grind the coffee. I already put the beans in the coffee grinder, and the water is about to boil," Mama said.

"Shhhh . . . listen to this." Papa had turned on the radio to hear that several students of the University of Munich had been executed because they had written and distributed leaflets, the so-called White Rose letters, against Hitler and written *"Nieder mit Hitler,"* Down with Hitler, on buildings near the university.

They were Hans Scholl, 25, a medical student, and his sister Sophie, 21, a biology student. Also guillotined with the Scholls was Christof Probst.

Only four days had elapsed from the day of their arrest until their execution. The execution took place on the same day as the sentencing.

Christof Probst could not say good-bye to anyone in his family. His wife, still confined with the birth of their third child, did not hear of his fate until after he had been executed.

These men had been allowed to attend classes at the University of Munich during the winter, while the fighting along the Russian front was suspended. In spring, they had to report back to the front in Russia. They had become disgusted with Hitler's tyranny, lies, and bloodshed. More than twenty other students, as well as one of their professors, were executed at a later date. The cream of the crop of the University of Munich was wiped out.

"This is one time I am glad that Ludwig was not yet at the university. Knowing how he hates war, I'm afraid he could have been one of them," Mama lamented. "Oh, those poor unfortunate young people. They didn't have a chance."

After Hans and Sophie Scholl's execution, their parents and their sister, Inge, were put in prison. Hitler had resurrected the *Sippenhaft,* the old Germanic tribal idea, which holds the whole family responsible for the actions of one of their members. It was yet another way to assure compliance through control and fear.

A little more than a year after the execution of the members of the White Rose, still another plot to kill Hitler, and thereby stop the bloodshed, took place.

Born November 15, 1907, Count Claus Schenk von Stauffenberg had a long military career. On the Russian front he was appalled by the murder of Jews by the SS, the treatment of the Russian civilian population, and atrocities against Russian POWs. By 1942, he knew that Hitler had to be overthrown. The Kreisau Circle, a group of top military men and civilians, plotted to kill Hitler.

On July 11, 1944, Colonel von Stauffenberg brought a bomb to a briefing at the Berghof, Hitler's mountain residence, but never had the opportunity to carry out the plan.

The next opportunity came on July 20, 1944. Colonel von Stauffenberg traveled to the *Wolfsschanze,* Wolf's Lair, in Prussia with his aide and co-conspirator, Lieutenant Werner von Heften. The plan was to place a bomb in an attaché case next to Hitler underneath the conference table.

The plot had been carefully planned, and it relied on the program *Unternehmen Walküre,* Operation Valkyrie, which Hitler himself had set up. The *Volkssturm,* Reserve Army, was to maintain order should anything happen to Hitler, or should riots break out. Only Hitler and General Friedrich Fromm, who was part of the plot, could set Operation Valkyrie in motion.

As soon as Hitler was dead, Fromm was to set Operation Valkyrie in motion, disarm the SS, and take over the large cities. Colonel von Stauffenberg set off the bomb, but, again, Hitler survived, with only his right arm injured.

Von Stauffenberg was captured after a desperate effort to set operation Valkyrie in motion. He was executed, without a trial, by a firing squad in the Courtyard of the War Ministry on July 21, 1944. (The movie "Valkyrie" was based on this plot.)

Like the execution of the members of the White Rose group, the radio and newspapers reported von Stauffenberg's execution to emphasize that any form of insurrection was punished immediately and severely.

Under Hitler's idea of *Sippenhaft,* von Stauffenberg's wife, Nina Schenk, Countess von Stauffenberg, was arrested and sent to the Ravensbruck Concentration camp. During her imprisonment, she gave birth to their fifth child, a daughter. Their four sons were sent to orphanages, and their family name was changed to "Meister." Hitler wanted the name von Stauffenberg obliterated.

Nina and all five of the children were able to survive until the end of the war, when they were reunited.

Claus von Stauffenberg's older brother Berthold, who also had supported the plot, was executed in the most inhumane way in the infamous Plötzensee Prison near Berlin-Charlottenburg.

Berthold's twin brother, Alexander Schenk von Stauffenberg, was fighting with the German Army in Greece. He was sent to Dachau, the concentration camp near Munich. He survived and was liberated on May 5, 1945, by the 5th U.S. Army in Tyrol, Austria, where the SS had abandoned its prisoners.

As a stone causes a ripple effect when thrown into water, so the Operation Valkyrie plot against Hitler caused a ripple effect resulting in hundreds of people being arrested and interrogated, and, more often than not, tortured and executed.

It was also in the Plötzensee Prison where other members of the Kreisau Circle were executed. It was Hitler himself who demanded that the remaining leaders of the July 20 plot should have a slow painful death. He ordered to have the executions filmed so he could watch as the conspirators were hung with piano wire on meat hooks.

Our family had a tangential relationship to one of those executed at Plötzensee because of his connection to von Stauffenberg. Before her marriage, Mama had worked for the family of the Countess von Marogna-Redwitz in Munich. While she had to work hard, she had good memories of her work for this family.

One member of the family, Count Rudolf von Marogna-Redwitz became acquainted with Count Claus von Stauffenberg around 1920 and later became a member of the circle around the count. He was sentenced to death by the *Volksgericht*, a kangaroo court, on October 12, 1944, and hanged at Plötzensee Prison on the same day.

After Hitler came to power, the number of executions in Germany increased dramatically from year to year. In 1940 alone, a record number of more than nine hundred German civilians were put to death for various "crimes" against the state. After 1941, the minimum age for execution in Germany was reduced to just fourteen years.

One did not have to be part of a resistance group to wind up in one of the mock courtrooms of the *Volksgericht*. Any negative remark against Hitler, the party, or the war was reason enough to be labeled an enemy of the State. In the *Volksgericht,* there was no chance for appeal; executions were often carried out the same day.

Elfriede Scholz, a pacifist novelist, serves as an example of how nebulous the reasons could be in determining who was an enemy of the state. She was the youngest sister of Erich Maria Remarque, author of the famous antiwar novel, "All Quiet on the Western Front." Erich Maria Remarque was in America, and the Nazis would have given anything to get their hands on him, but they could not, so they got to him through his sister.

At her sentencing, Elfriede Scholz was told by the infamous Judge Roland Freisler, *"Ihr Bruder ist uns entwischt, aber Sie werden uns nicht entwischen!"*—"Your brother has escaped us, but you will not escape us!" She was beheaded in Plötzensee Prison on December 16, 1943.

In another case, a gifted musician became the victim of the Nazi's zealous prosecution of so-called enemies of the state.

Karlrobert Kreiten, at age 27, was one of the most talented pianists in Germany at the time. At age eleven, he had made his debut in a live broadcast. When he made some negative remarks about Hitler and the war effort, his neighbor turned him in to the Gestapo. He was executed on September 7, 1943, in Plötzensee by hanging.

The executions that took place at this one prison—Plötzensee—exemplify the ruthlessness the regime used to instill fear and curb resistance. In the 42 years from 1890 to 1932, the prison had only 36 executions, mostly for murder. Under Hitler, in 12 years from 1933 to 1945, more than 2,500 people—"enemies" of the state—were executed there by the verdict of the *Volksgericht.*

No wonder the average person felt helpless in the face of such senseless and calculated brutality.

With all of the attempts to kill Hitler or to resist his stranglehold on Germany, it is uncanny how he was able to escape with his life again and again and to maintain his power until Germany was destroyed.

Hitler, indeed, seemed to have more than nine lives. But his nine lives came with a terrible price for the thousands who dared to oppose him and for the population at large whom he oppressed.

About the Author

Anneliese Heider Tisdale was born in Munich, Germany, and lived there through World War II. After the war, she worked as an interpreter for the U.S. Military Government.

In 1947, she came to the United States as a war bride and became a U.S. citizen on November 20, 1950. After earning bachelor's and master's degrees from the University of Iowa, she taught foreign languages in public schools in Cedar Rapids, Iowa, for almost 30 years.

Anneliese and her husband, Jim, live in Cedar Rapids. She is the mother of three and the "bonus" mother of four. She enjoys her grandchildren and great-grandchildren, and they enjoy her cooking.

This memoir is her first book. She is now at work on a second book about her experiences adjusting to her new country.